Doing Justice

Critical South

The publication of this series is supported by the International Consortium of Critical Theory Programs funded by the Andrew W. Mellon Foundation.

Series editors: Natalia Brizuela and Leticia Sabsay

Leonor Arfuch, *Memory and Autobiography*
Aimé Césaire, *Resolutely Black*
Bolívar Echeverría, *Modernity and "Whiteness"*
Celso Furtado, *The Myth of Economic Development*
Eduardo Grüner, *The Haitian Revolution*
María Pia López, *Not One Less*
Pablo Oyarzun, *Doing Justice*
Néstor Perlongher, *Plebeian Prose*
Nelly Richard, *Eruptions of Memory*
Silvia Rivera Cusicanqui, *Ch'ixinakax Utxiwa*
Tendayi Sithole, *The Black Register*

Doing Justice

Three Essays on Walter Benjamin

Pablo Oyarzun

Translated by Stephen Gingerich

polity

Excerpt from *Walter Benjamin: Selected Writings, Volume 2, 1927-1934*, translated by Rodney Livingstone and Others, edited by Michael W. Jennings, Howard Eiland, and Gary Smith, Cambridge, Mass.: The Belknap Press of Harvard University Press. Copyright © 1999 by the President and Fellows of Harvard College.

Polity Press
65 Bridge Street
Cambridge CB2 1UR, UK

Polity Press
101 Station Landing
Suite 300
Medford, MA 02155, USA

ISBN-13: 978-1-5095-4197-3- hardback
ISBN-13: 978-1-5095-4198-0- paperback

A catalogue record for this book is available from the British Library.

Library of Congress Cataloging-in-Publication Data

Names: Oyarzun R., Pablo, 1950- author. | Gingerich, Stephen, translator.
Title: Doing justice : three essays on Walter Benjamin / Pablo Oyarzun ; translated by Stephen Gingerich.
Other titles: Tres ensayos sobre Benjamin. English
Description: Cambridge ; Medford, MA : Polity, [2020] | Series: Critical south | Includes bibliographical references and index. | Summary: "A leading Latin American thinker examines the work of Walter Benjamin and demonstrates its relevance for our understanding of justice"-- Provided by publisher.
Identifiers: LCCN 2020005429 (print) | LCCN 2020005430 (ebook) | ISBN 9781509541973 (hardback) | ISBN 9781509541980 (paperback) | ISBN 9781509541997 (epub) | ISBN 9781509543779 (pdf)
Subjects: LCSH: Benjamin, Walter, 1892-1940--Political and social views. | Benjamin, Walter, 1892-1940--Criticism and interpretation. | Justice in literature.
Classification: LCC PT2603.E455 Z79356 2020 (print) | LCC PT2603.E455 (ebook) | DDC 838/.91209--dc23
LC record available at https://lccn.loc.gov/2020005429
LC ebook record available at https://lccn.loc.gov/2020005430

Typeset in 11 on 13pt Sabon Lt Pro
by Fakenham Prepress Solutions, Fakenham, Norfolk NR21 8NL
Printed and bound in Great Britain by TJ International Limited

For further information on Polity, visit our website:
politybooks.com

Contents

Note on the Texts

The author has published translations into Spanish of many works by Walter Benjamin, including most of the work discussed in this volume. (These editions have been included in the bibliography.) The original Spanish text therefore integrates his own translations with references to standard German editions of Benjamin's work, and often includes the original German text when this is appropriate for his interpretation and commentary. The translator has chosen to preserve the German interpolations and to include, when possible, references to both the German editions and the standard English translation, using in the text the abbreviations listed here in order to reduce the number of bibliographic notes. Occasionally, the English translation has been altered and made to harmonize with Oyarzun's interpretation; such modifications, wholly the responsibility of the translator, are noted parenthetically, as translator's notes (TNs). Translations from German, when a text is not available in English, are the translator's; they take into account the author's Spanish version. When given in the text, the sigla listed below will include a Roman numeral indicating the volume and, when necessary, an Arabic numeral indicating the section, followed by page numbers.

A   Walter Benjamin. *Arcades Project*, translated by Howard Eiland and Kevin McLaughlin. Belknap Press of Harvard University Press, 1999.

GS   Walter Benjamin. *Gesammelte Schriften*, edited by Rolf Tiedemann and Hermann Schweppenhäuser. Suhrkamp, 1991. 14 volumes.

O   Walter Benjamin. *Origin of the German Trauerspiel*, translated by Howard Eiland. Harvard University Press, 2019.

SW   Walter Benjamin. *Selected Writings*, edited by Marcus Bullock and Michael W. Jennings. Belknap Press of Harvard University Press, 1996. 4 volumes.

WN   Walter Benjamin. *Werke und Nachlaß: Kritische Gesamtausgabe*, edited by Christoph Gödde and Henri Lonitz. Suhrkamp, 2010. 21 volumes.

Introduction
"...beneath these clouds"

Jacques Lezra

Are we truly, though, midway to making real what ought to be, as the historical discourse of the winners insists? If we pass a hand over that well-groomed story—but do so against the part and against the grain, as Walter Benjamin counseled—won't it perhaps turn out that what this history holds to be "exceptional"—exceptions that constantly and forcefully occur, even in our days—can teach us more regarding the history of democracy in modernity, and about its current possibilities, than what that history recognizes as the "rule"?

Bolívar Echeverría, "El sentido del siglo XX"

beneath these clouds, in a field of force of destructive torrents and explosions, was the tiny, fragile human body.

Benjamin

Cuento is the name given to the bolster used to shore up what threatens to fall into ruins; hence the expression *andar, o estar en cuentos*, to be or find oneself *en cuentos*: to be in danger, and hold oneself together with handiwork and artifice.

Covarrubias, *Tesoro de la lengua castellana, o española*

How, who, what is Walter Benjamin "in Latin America"?[1] What did and what does Benjamin teach Latin America? So asked a helpful collection of essays from 2010.[2] For Benjamin's influence in Mexico, Chile, Argentina, Brazil and elsewhere, in Portuguese and Spanish translation, though read in German and English as well, has been profound. His "Theses on the Philosophy of History" help Michael Löwy understand the theology of liberation that takes hold distinctively across the continent.[3] Benjamin's "For a Critique of Violence"—first in Héctor Murena's 1967 version *del alemán*, "from the German," then in a faulty translation by Jesús Aguirre, and most recently translated from German in 2007–2008 by Pablo Oyarzun and republished in 2017 in a revised edition, with an accompanying group of essays by distinguished Latin American philosophers—serves to organize the Latin American response to the failures and successes of revolutionary movements, from Central America to the Southern Cone. A *Glosario Walter Benjamin: Conceptos y figuras* was published in Mexico in 2016. Benjamin is studied from the perspective of exile and, in Brazil, of the philosophy and practices of translation. He shapes the understanding of Latin American literary and artistic modernism.[4] He helps define what has been called the *barroco de indias*. He is read against, and with, authors such as Mariátegui, Bolivar Echeverría, *Óscar del Barco, and Viveiros de Castro*. He is received in agonistic relation to Derrida, Agamben, Hamacher and others—each also read differently, in the publishing and scholarly markets that run from Mexico to Brazil, from how they are read in Europe or the United States. And, of course, the reception of Walter Benjamin has differed depending on the institutional and political cultures in which each country has read him and on the moment and circumstance of each country. Reading Benjamin is a different matter under Pinochet from what it is under the long rule of the Institutional Revolutionary Party in Mexico; it is one thing to read the "Theses on the Philosophy of History" under Videla in Argentina and quite another to hear news of it in Havana, where Benjamin had once hoped to find himself, with Theodor Adorno's help. Latin American Marxisms—which do not map easily onto the European varieties—take on Benjamin's texts with different degrees of reluctance, violence, enthusiasm, and misprision—or reject them, again, for various reasons.

What does the complex, controversial, partial, rich, differentiated reception of Benjamin in Latin America offer anglophone readers of Benjamin's work? And why now? Why offer *now*, in English, these essays about Walter Benjamin written by one of Latin America's foremost philosophers, translators, and essayists? There is one answer for both questions: partly because Pablo Oyarzun's *Doing Justice* will help an anglophone readership understand what it means to take account of, and to be responsible for and to, the "now."[5] What is it about *today*, just now, that requires thought, particularly the thought of those whose world is made up in, and of, English—the language of global capital at the moment of its crisis, in other words *now*? I'll say that crisis is not *a moment*; that *every* moment is critical; that the relation that thought bears to crisis is a matter of justice, of doing justice to, in, and through crisis, of justly *translating* crisis: I can move through these assertions, from one to the next, stepwise, in the wake of Benjamin's work. I arrive at the last one: I find Pablo Oyarzun's work waiting.

I want to be careful, though. What Oyarzun's essays offer the anglophone reader now is inseparably related to his writing about Benjamin *in Spanish*. That, though, was not these essays' goal when they appeared in Spanish and helped to form Benjamin's reception by Latin America's Spanish-speaking readership. Rather the opposite: Pablo Oyarzun's essays were intended to provide an alternative—in Spanish, with Latin America as a backdrop, a goal, and a resource—*to* the industry of Benjamin

readings in English, French, and German, flowing South
in translation or in the original from New York, or
Paris, or Berlin. For this reason, a translation of Pablo
Oyarzun's work should have the constant company of
disarming questions: what does it mean to write in Spanish
about works from a philosophical tradition from which
Spanish has long been excluded? How does the value
that a moment ("now"), or a state, or a complex cultural
prejudice assigns to a language like Spanish affects how its
philosophers can make claims? How does such a language
describe? How true can it hope to be? (Even phrasing the
question this way proves violent. We think it means: Can
the generality of a thesis' truth claims be separated from
the language in which these claims are articulated? But in
Castilian Spanish we would say: ¿*Cuán verdadera puede
esperar ser?* and we bring time, waiting, *esperar,* into
the expression. In Spanish, I wait where I hope; less so,
much less so, in English. The burning question of philosophical untranslatability... To the anglophone world,
Spanish remains largely a servile language—the language
of abjection, of *la bestia*; the language spoken on the other
side of the wall; the language of the European PIGS—
Portugal, Italy, Greece, and Spain. In the age of Donald
Trump, to reach for a philosophical timbre in Spanish will
appear to some degree improper, or an act of defiance.
These senses of Spanish are to be noted and understood
as conditions of philosophical expression *now*, when
the relation between Latin America and the anglophone
world enters a different world, a world globalized utterly
differently from heretofore, in the wake of the COVID-19
pandemic.

Marx and Freud, Foucault said, founded discursiv-
ities; we might say that they were world making. As is
Benjamin. A work, as well as the novel interpretation of a
work or of a significant body of work, can make a world
other, break it, unfound the discourse that composes it,
and reconfigure it around the displacement of what was

already assimilated and around all the emplacements that emerge *now*, in light of the new. The world of Walter Benjamin's work has its rhythms, its crystallizations on different focal terms: violence; mysticism; law; allegory; history. These terms set values in different academic and non-academic markets and travel with greater or less ease from one language to another. *Gewalt* offers a sort of value, and offers it differently in the French academic context from how it offers it in the American or the Italian one; "violence" offers another, and differently in Santiago from in New York. And so on, at different times, with consequences that change and reconfigure past worlds, as well as what we imagine to be the case and what will come.

I say that the interpretation of a significant body of work makes a world other. This is hardly news. Any number of examples will come to mind; to choose a single one, or even a number, is to configure a world in which that sort of example has a normative weight. I'll be offering the name "Benjamin," for instance, as a sort of metonym: his name stands for other names, which stand for works that also make worlds new and make new worlds, when read out of place and against their time. This is familiar ground, well covered by subaltern studies and articulated recently in the languages of the so-called decolonial option. Yes, when Benjamin's body of work passes through the South, through peripheral readings, through the capitals of the twenty-first century rather than of the nineteenth, or even twentieth, when it takes shape in the languages of the South, then the focal terms that arrange its values change sense, and the worlds they configure change too. Both suffer translations. What terms and worlds suffer will make up other worlds than those in which Walter Benjamin was first read and valued and received. The North (my caricature, of course) will be reading Benjamin through, and in, contexts for which his work was not explicitly intended. The South will no longer read Walter

Benjamin as the bearer of European legitimacy. Like that famous word-laden suitcase that he carried to Port Bou, Benjamin will now have been lost—lost to the fantasy that his work bears *to* Europe, *for* Europe, the last illumination of European enlightenment (and that it bears to those it is *not* for, *to* the colony, just its shadows or reflections); and lost to the fantasy that his work, always already estranged from its original habitat, finds itself at home— or less unhoused—somewhere at the periphery, in Buenos Aires or in Santiago or in Johannesburg. Now, the boulevards and parks of Paris are distressed by, mapped on, the *grandes alamedas*, the great shaded avenues of (say) Santiago de Chile—and vice-versa.

But Walter Benjamin's work, read in and from the South, seems to me particularly addressed to this moment, just for what escapes its representativeness, its metonymy; just for what makes that, vice versa, spurious. (Here is Benjamin's difference: I have to say what "this moment" is, or what I take it to be; to whom his work sets on "offer" what escapes representativeness; I am responsible for addressing its address. This, I think, is what *Jetztzeit* entails.)[6] Take this example. It's phrase that recalls a moment like the one we are living *now*, when one world was unmade, and another announced—abortively, incompletely. Pablo Oyarzun opens *Doing Justice* by remarking: "An experience always overflows its context." He is thinking about experiences we—he, history—seek to foreclose: "never again," we say, for instance (it is not just any example), regarding *los desaparecidos*, "the disappeared." For Oyarzun, the circumstance that gives rise to the injunction "never again" is not single. He recalls Salvador Allende's words on September 11, 1973—*Sigan ustedes sabiendo que, mucho más temprano que tarde, de nuevo [se] abrirán las grandes alamedas por donde pase el hombre libre para construir una sociedad mejor*—the conventional translation of which would be "Do not stop knowing that, much sooner than later, the great shaded

avenues will open again, down which free men will walk
to build a better society." Oyarzun tells us that it took
him forty years to understand that Allende's sentence did
not lack the reflexive pronoun *se*, as in my conventional
translation—[*se*] *abrirán*, "the great shaded avenues will
reopen, will open themselves, will be opened"—but rather
that the sentence embedded a promise and an injunction:
the people of Chile, to whom the sentence is addressed, are
enjoined into political subjectivity: *Sigan ustedes sabiendo*,
"Continue to know," or perhaps "Continue, progress,
move forward, and do so knowing that sooner or later
you will open for yourselves the great avenues," or even
"Press on in and by means of the knowledge that one day
you will open *for yourselves* the great avenues..."

Forty years, Oyarzun tells us, separate the experience
from his understanding. That period installed in Chile
what he calls *el régimen más despiadado del "se"* and
la equivocidad aciaga del "se"—which English can only
render, rather poorly, as something like "the pitiless
regime of the impersonal reflexive passive *se*" or "the
fateful equivocity of the passive voice." The impersonal
reflexive passive erased Allende's addressee. Where his
call to the people of Chile beat implicitly, the regime
installed the hegemonizing braid of political coercion,
consensus, and (self-)knowledge that the homonymy of
se carries. Poetically, with the vertiginous speed of the
pun rather than the forty-year delay, the forty years of
waiting with which it reaches Pablo Oyarzun (and us):
an overdetermined number, Moses's number, the number
of waiting in the desert, the number of exile—poetically,
the impersonal reflexive passive particle *se* tells us *se sabe*,
"it's generally known" (the coercion of consensus); it says
the verbal form *sé*, "I know" (the unassailable assertion: I
know what I know); and it speaks the imperative *sé*, "be!"
(In Castilian Spanish we say ¡*Sé bueno*!, "Be good!"; and
we translate רוֹא יְהִי or *sit lux* [*Vetus Latina*] and *fiat lux*
[*Vulgata*] as "¡*Que se haga la luz!* or *!Sea la luz!*") Like a

call he now hears ringing under the "fateful equivocity" of *se*, against the hegemonizing coupling of political coercion and (self-)knowledge that anchored Pinochet's regime, Oyarzun offers what he and others *should* have heard in 1973, what all Chile should have heard: Allende's proper audience, the political subject that Allende sought to call into being by promising the collective addressee its future. Here Benjamin is Oyarzun's—and Latin America's—guide.

> *Benjamin se esforzó por echar luz sobre lo que aquí llamo la equivocidad aciaga del "se," discernir en él todo vestigio de lo demónico—esa otra impersonalidad revestida de figuras vengativas, caprichosas y violentas, presta a retornar en todo momento con la parafernalia o la insidia del "siempre, una y otra vez"—discernir, digo, lo demónico de una violencia radicalmente distinta, que se borra a sí misma en el instante mismo en que se desencadena, porque emancipa. Las huellas de este afán siguen presentes en toda su obra.*

Benjamin attempted to illuminate what I call here the fateful equivocity of the passive voice and to highlight in it all vestiges of the demonic—this other impersonality wrapped up as it is in vindictive, whimsical, and violent figures and poised to return at any moment, with the paraphernalia or malicious claim of an "always, again and again." In other words, Benjamin wanted to differentiate demonic violence from a radically different kind of violence, one that is erased in the very instant in which it is unleashed, because it has emancipatory force. This ambition has left traces on his entire oeuvre. (Prologue, pp. xix–xx)

What do we make of the forty-year lag between the event and the experience on the one hand, and their interpretation on the other? Of the antithetical value of *se*—fatefully, dreadfully equivocal, but also demonic or daemonic, Oyarzun says (and we are to take *daimon* in its double sense: the insidious, the evil, the diabolical, but also the figure of philosophical integrity that calls the wandering thinker—call him Socrates—back to the just path, the path of truth). *Se*, coercively hegemonizing, but diagnostic and critical at the same time? A *se* that hides, disappears, buries the collective political subjectivity that Allende promised and sought to bring into being; but also one that, forty or fifty years later, can violently bring it forth: *sea el pueblo de Chile, sé?*

Minimally, three things.

First, the event, never coincident with experience or interpretation, can eventually come into being, or even be commanded into being *(¡sé!)*.[7] Forty years pass; knowledge (*saber*, to know: *yo sé*, "I know") catches up with the event of Allende's radio transmission; the event of his promise to the people of Chile discloses itself (in Castilian, *se revela*, "it reveals itself") to Pablo Oyarzun. Now Oyarzun can say, "I know to whom Allende's phrase was addressed"; *sé quiénes [se] abrirán las grandes alamedas.* Let's call "redemption" the horizon of possibility that opens when, and since, an event does not disclose itself as one and does not come into being at one time. (I am reading Oyarzun's reading of Benjamin through and with Adorno, whose suspicion of singularity I share.) The standpoint of redemption: that an event a world ago can be called into being: *sé; sea el pueblo de Chile.* And this retrospective calling into being operates according to what Oyarzun calls "a radically different kind of violence, one that is erased [*se borra*] in the very instant in which it is unleashed [= unleashes itself, *se desencadena*], because it has emancipatory force." Oyarzun rightly gives this "radically different kind of violence" its proper name: justice, *Gerechtigkeit*. The possibility of redeeming the event, the always open possibility of encountering or making a different addressee and of making appear a different world for the event of an enunciation, is the condition of (its) justice.[8]

Second, we encounter this non-coincidence of the event with experience and with interpretation where a natural language's substances (names, nouns, pronouns) touch on its times, on its tenses, on its verbs, on its eventuality. Where there is predication, there the event may be redeemed, and there justice may be done. And this means not only attending, as Oyarzun does with exemplary care, with the care of a translator and a philosopher, to Benjamin's language; even more importantly, it also means committing ourselves to reading one natural language's predications through and against another's. German through and in Spanish; this English sentence I am writing, in and against Spanish. Each has its times; for each, predication installs a relation the subject bears to truth and to the event that another language can only paraphrase. To do justice to English is to install in it another language's times and truths. Another language's world is the condition of a language's *se*.

The English language and Benjamin's German parse their reflexive, passive, and impersonal constructions— their autopredications, the instants at which something like a reflexive position emerges in a language with respect to itself; its *se*-moments; the places and times where I act upon myself, or where an impersonal act carries the weight of a historical event—differently from Spanish, indeed differently from Romance languages in general. This is how Allende's words have been translated into German. Note the reflexive, impersonal formation *sich auftun werden* for *se abrirán*.

> *Werktätige meines Vaterlandes! Ich glaube an Chile und sein Schicksal. Es werden andere Chilenen kommen. In diesen düsteren und bitteren Augenblicken, in denen sich der Verrat durchsetzt, sollt ihr wissen, dass sich früher oder später, sehr bald, erneut die großen Straßen auftun werden, auf denen der würdige Mensch dem Aufbau einer besseren Gesellschaft entgegengeht.*[9]

In English:

> Workers of my country, I have faith in Chile and its destiny. Other men will overcome this dark and bitter moment when

treason seeks to prevail. Keep in mind that, much sooner than later, great avenues will again open, through which will pass the free man, to construct a better society.[10]

Oyarzun's Benjamin is least familiar to the English-speaking world just here. In both English and German, the daemonic *se*-moment and the interval between event, experience, and articulation (the retrospective articulation of Allende's interpellation of the Chilean people into political subjectivity) are foreclosed—so much so, indeed, that the German translation reaches for its object and calls out *andere Chilenen* by name just where Allende's Spanish leaves the announced political subject as yet nameless. No language, not English, not German, not Spanish, can *do justice* to the event; but could Oyarzun have come to the story of waiting, hope, and political interpellation that Spanish offers him without reading Allende's words *through* the in-justice that English and German do, each in its way, to the event, the experience, and their articulation?

In this sense, then: third, doing justice is indeed, along with *Doing Justice*, a matter of translation. This is why I'll be running the risk of translating Oyarzun's concern today—his concern with "doing justice," with that "doing" that is *claiming* or *demanding* justice, with narration and justice in Benjamin's work—into a matter that also matters to me—the matter of translation—but that would appear to be extrinsic to the immediate concerns of *Doing Justice*. I risk seeming to play irresponsibly, unjustly, with Pablo Oyarzun's words by translating the problem of articulating narrating and justice into the problem of articulating translating and justice. Where Oyarzun subtly and convincingly tells the story of the narrator's vocation for justice, you'll fear to hear me say something like "Justice is a matter of translation," or "Translation is a matter of justice, of doing justice."

The questions how justice is to be done and how justice is to be demanded are Pablo Oyarzun's topic.

He approaches these desperately timely questions by shifting focus—for Latin America as well as for the anglophone world—from the famous essays "For a Critique of Violence," "The Work of Art in the Age of its Technical Reproducibility," and "The Task of the Translator" (essays definitive of Benjamin's reception in Latin America and the United States) to the analysis of Walter Benjamin's essay "The Storyteller," called in Spanish "El narrador."[11] Let me attend to two sentences that mark this shift. The first is Pablo Oyarzun's summary definition of the specific character of narrative, of the story, with regard to Justice: "The righteous character of storytelling," he says, "consists in giving an account of the happening of the singular, that is, in giving an account of what is singular in its happening" (p. 105)—or, in Spanish, *El carácter justiciero de la narración consiste en que ella da cuenta del acaecer de lo singular, es decir, da cuenta de lo singular en su acaecer.* *Justiciero* is hard to translate—it means "justice doing," but with a strong connotation of severity, of meting out justice with exemplary severity. The second is a sentence I take from the very end of this volume. Oyarzun recapitulates his argument.

> *Como tantos otros textos de Benjamin, y podría decirse aun como un rasgo indeleble de su escritura, este ensayo hace además de celar un secreto cuya revelación destruiría por completo su fuerza de verdad. Una débil fuerza, entonces, como aquella de la que habla "Sobre el concepto de la historia". Esta débil fuerza—que es aquella y sólo aquella requerida por la justicia— es, acaso, la que trama a la vez la narración del narrador y el texto de Benjamin. Es como si en la contextura general del ensayo, en sus vectores argumentales, en su repertorio de imágenes y ejemplos y giros, en suma, en su estilo, se estuviese dando cuenta de lo que el mismo ensayo atribuye a la narración.*

As do so many other texts by Benjamin—so that we might even say that this is an indelible trait of his writing—["The

Storyteller"] gives the impression of guarding a secret whose revelation would completely destroy the force of its truth. It is a weak power, then, like the one "The Concept of History" speaks about. This weak power—which is the one and only one required for justice—might well be the power that weaves together both the story of the storyteller and Benjamin's text. It is as if what the essay itself—in its general fabric, in its argumentative vectors and its repertoire of images and its examples, its twists and turns, in short, in its style—says about storytelling gave an account of itself. (Chapter 3, p. 107)

Here again the translation is tricky, and I'll return to it—in this case, to the expression *Es como si ... en su estilo, se estuviese dando cuenta*, which is not exactly, and not only, "It is as if... in its style, what the essay itself says about storytelling gave an account of itself." The verbal form *dar cuenta* crops up in both cases, in the first sentence I quoted and in this last one: it can be translated "to give account" or "to render an account." It is as if the philosopher gives an account, *dar cuenta*, or a *reckoning* of what the storyteller recounts: the Spanish verb is *contar cuenta*. And it is as though, at the close of Oyarzun's *Doing Justice*, this account of a telling, this reckoning of telling, has a twist: *Es como si... en su estilo, se estuviese dando cuenta*. It is as though, in its style, it—but what? Or who?—were *realizing, becoming aware*, of what the essay itself attributes to the story. The work became its daemon. *Darse cuenta*: to realize, to come into reckoning with, though reflexively: *dar-se*, to give oneself the reckoning.

I'll come back to these two sentences, but take away from them this: first, the uncomfortable joining of attention to singularity with the *exemplary* severity with which the "righteous" pay that attention, the exemplary severity of the bearer of the sword of justice. And, second, the essay's drift *from* taking account *to* giving oneself, or itself, the reckoning. This movement, this drift, is a figure of coming to awareness or noticing. Its span is not forty years long;

this drift, this movement, is to be accomplished in and by means of *Doing Justice*: it is, indeed, the condition on which justice is done. But the caesura between these two moments also blocks—opens an unbridgeable gulf between—the force of a law based on taking account, on empiricism, on nature and noting and a form of justice based on giving an account of oneself.[12]

Oyarzun begins with the observation that Benjamin's concern "is the destruction of experience as a result of the unfolding, in modernity, of technology that culminates in war." He says:

> The development of the argument of "The Storyteller" offers convincing proof … that Benjamin considers the process of destruction compendiously. It is not a *type* of experience, but rather experience itself that is devastated by this process. But with this devastation something that belongs to the core of experience itself seems to get irremissibly lost, something that artisanal storytelling continues to protect like a dear treasure, something that is not substantive in itself but has the subtlety of a disposition, of fortitude and care, of attentiveness (*Aufmerksamkeit*). This something is the vocation of justice that inspires storytelling. [*Ese algo es la vocación de justicia que anima a la narración.*] (Chapter 3, p. 76; my emphasis)

I hardly need to underscore the urgency that beats here, which Oyarzun reads clearly in Benjamin's words. "Never," writes Benjamin at the beginning of "The Storyteller,"

> has experience been contradicted more thoroughly than strategic experience by tactical warfare, economic experience by inflation, bodily experience by mechanical warfare, moral experience by those in power. A generation that had gone to school on a horse-drawn streetcar now stood under the open sky in a countryside in which nothing remained unchanged but the clouds, and beneath these clouds, in a field of force of destructive torrents and explosions, was the tiny, fragile human body. (Harry Zohn's translation)

The "field of force of destructive torrents and explosions" acutely assaulted and definitively changed the soldiers who were traveling home from World War I's battlefields. The "destruction of experience" of which war is a type—the bloodiest, the most acute—is, for Benjamin, modernity's condition and result. It is the condition on which capital trades accelerated consumption for use and habitation; and it is the effect of that trade. Planetary war—by which we now mean suicidal war with the planet, with the environment—is the evident successor to world wars, bloodier still, more acute even than the most acute of world wars. And, in a way that speaks both to the problem of scale—that is, to the terrible problem of the relation between justice and scale—and to the problem of kind—that is, to the terrible logic of the symbolic and material inequality of the "tiny, fragile" bodies, things, and creatures "under the open sky"—this planetary war is more unjust still than even the exterminating wars that make up human history.

Hence the urgency of the questions how justice is to be done and how justice is to be demanded.

We want first a practical answer; we want something that is "substantive in itself," as Oyarzun writes (p. 76), and, if not that, we want at least a pronoun, an indication. *Who* will do justice—the prophet, the philosopher, the lawmaker, the activist, the storyteller? *Who* demands it, in *whose* name, and *what* will we be redressing, remediating, distributing?

But Benjamin and Oyarzun slow us down, in ways that my response here and now is unable, for practical reasons, to do more than note.

Just what is "the vocation of justice," *la vocación de justicia*, that inspires or animates storytelling? A vocation is, of course, a calling. It is generally felt as an inner call, though this calling somehow chimes with a different sort of voice; and this chiming, this rhyming of the inner voice that calls me to something with a profession or a task, this chiming of my inner voice with something of a different order is what makes my vocation different from an appetite, for example, or from my desire, or from a whim. It is what distinguishes vocation from what in Castilian Spanish we'd call *un capricho*. I mentioned that I may feel called to a profession or to a task. I will say that teaching is my vocation, or that translating is the task to which I am called. When I attend to the call of my vocation I take account both of what is interior to me, which is of the order of what I want or fancy; and also of what, other than what is subjective in me and for me, rhymes with it but is of a different order. If I attend doubly in this way, I will have rhymed myself with, or also attended to, what is other than myself. I won't call this vocation of the other than myself "objective" or "transcendental," although we might say that the term "vocation" takes account of both. I'll say that I will have rhymed myself with what is other than myself by taking account of what is other than my voice to myself, other than my conscience; that I will have brought myself to rhyme. And sometimes I will follow one rather than the other of these sketchily defined voices, and eventually find myself in the wrong profession, or performing a task that is not my calling.

Now, to answer to *any* vocation, it would seem, is to take account of what calls me other than my voice in me—the vocation to be a teacher, the call to become a translator. If it is not to be my whim, then any vocation takes account of what is other than my voice in me. But how will I know that my vocation is *not* just whim, or fancy? What I called "my voice in me," my conscience or my desire inasmuch as these are subjective expressions, speaks to me now; but whatever it is that rhymes with it speaks out of that time, in a different tense. When I act on my desire but in time to the time of the vocation of the other in me, I'm bringing my *now* into rhyme, rhythmically, with a different time. I fancy now, but my vocation proves itself in the event; its tense is perfective.

This, I think, is generally true, whether I'm attending to the call of justice or to that of a profession—the call to nurse, to care, to be a payer of attention, to teach, to tell stories, what have you. But the vocation of justice is also of a different order again: it is not a *type* of taking account of what is other in me; the vocation of justice is not a profession among others except in the sense that to be called into justice and to respond is to profess.

Rather, justice *is* this taking account of what is other than me in me: it is the structure of all and any vocation. Justice is responsible to what is perfectly expressed now, my desire, and to what remains perfective.

To ask how justice is to be done now, today, in desperate urgency, when we are threatened by the "devastation" of experience, is to ask how we take account of what is other than ourselves in ourselves: so Benjamin says, as Pablo Oyarzun explains. "But with this devastation something that belongs to the core of experience itself seems to get irremissibly lost." And now, faced with this "devastation," "artisanal storytelling continues to protect [the vocation of justice] like a dear treasure." This "vocation," Oyarzun's Benjamin says, "is not substantive in itself but has the subtlety of a disposition, of fortitude and care, of attentiveness (*Aufmerksamkeit*)" (p. 76).

"Narration and Justice." Perhaps this would be a way into (an Introduction to) a response to *Doing Justice*—the acknowledgment or the hypothesis of a special relation between the demand for justice, the demand that justice be done, and timeliness. By "timeliness" I would be designating something about the nature of the demand for justice: it is of a time; it requires something of us in time, *on* time. The demand is articulated in the present tense: we demand action on climate justice *right now*, in the name of the future (in this case), or in the name of damage done in the past (reparations). The demand, though, is paradoxical in at least this sense—that whatever we do or imagine doing in response to the demand for justice is not held to what justice is now, when it is demanded of us or when we demand it of another or of ourselves; now, when we can articulate what we believe is just just now; now, when we are doing justice by doing what we represent to ourselves as just. Instead, whatever we are doing when we are doing justice to the demand is held to the standard of what justice *will have been* just now. A different tense makes itself felt just here. Once upon a time, I say, "A different tense makes itself felt," or "Once upon a time, a different tense will have made itself felt." I might say that the storyteller tells the story of the perpetual battle between these different tenses, and that the storyteller's story is just, or does justice, to the degree that no tense triumphs, or becomes the story's protagonist.

This is all rather allegorical, so let me be clearer as I move to close.

Recall the questions that lie behind Pablo Oyarzun's title, the questions of what it means to "do justice" and to "demand justice." "Doing justice" translates the expression *hacer justicia*, which in Castilian or Chilean Spanish is an infinitive expression: "to do justice." In Spanish the infinitive lends itself to substantivization more easily than the English does—we say *el hacer justicia*, "the doing justice" or "the to do justice"—and can make that noun the subject of a clause like *es imposible el hacer justicia*, "the doing of justice is impossible," which can be shorn of the pronoun to leave *es imposible hacer justicia*, a common nominal clause.

Of the philosophically non-trivial differences between the verbs *hacer* and "to do" remark just these two.

We say *hacer* in Spanish when we speak of *making* something—its etymology links it to the Latin *facere*, to produce, create, fabricate. The relation between *facere* and what is made, *factum*, and what is fabricated, *fictio* (< *fingere*), is well enough known—"fact" and "fiction," *hecho* and *hechura*, this last the Castilian version of *poiema*, a "fashioning"; for example, man is God's poem in Ephesians 2:10. Is justice, then, something *hecho*, something that is made, fashioned? Is justice a fashioning, a construction—contingent, made out of this or that material in someone's hands at this moment, and out of something different, in another's hands at another moment? Is justice different as it travels from hand to hand, or as the word travels from mouth to mouth, from one story-teller's mouth to another's? Is justice thus something that can be *un*fashioned, something of the order of the deconstructible? If justice can be *hecha*, it can be *deshecha*, when for instance *un desfacedor de agravios* like don Quixote is asked to undo an injustice that had appeared to some, at some time, to be justice. We are accustomed to granting that law is *made* or fabricated; about justice, though, the stories we tell are mixed. Justice is divine, a deity; it is irreducible and undeconstructible; it is the condition on which the law stands and the standard to which laws are held. A law can be unjust—and we will petition for redress, seek to change it, or seek to pass another, a just law. To refuse to obey an unjust law, though, puts us into contravention, not just of a law, but of justice—and this, at least, Socrates will not do. Are we ready to characterize this solemn principle as a *fabrication*? Even, tendentially, as *fiction*?

Note also this.

Hacer, I said, is infinitive. "Doing" justice, in English, speaks to us of dynamics in the present, of a present progressiveness: it is what we are, or should be, *doing*. Justice, as Pablo Oyarzun showed us, is not done; maybe justice is never done; it is imperfective, imperfectible. But the expression "doing justice" exists notwithstanding—we understand, roughly, imperfectly, what it means now, or what it is meaning. It is in the doing of justice that justice is poorly, unjustly imagined, or named, or presented. Let's flip the poor phrase: justice is presented in doing justice. We should maybe even intensify the paradox: justice is just what is presented in doing justice. When we lose the passive we are *almost* in the familiar, cold grip of tautology: we *do* justice when we *do* justice. Doing justice regarding this or that circumstance also does the "justice" to which our doing justice will then refer. It also "does" the work of making that to which the word "justice" will refer.

When we ask what it means to *do justice*, we immediately ask after the matter of tense: doing justice does what we will refer to when we say that we are doing, will be doing, or have done justice.

We are onto something here, in English, that bears on the definition of justice, and Pablo Oyarzun helps us to it, helps us see what English *does*—and what the Spanish infinitive *hacer* does not do. We might say: Pablo Oyarzun's reading, in English translation, from his Spanish, of Benjamin's German about the translation into German by Johannes von Guenther from the Russian of Nikolai Leskov helps do justice to what English *is doing* whenever "doing" translates *hacer*; and it helps us see where Spanish fails to do justice.

Now remember Pablo Oyarzun's summary definition of the character of the story with regard to Justice: "The righteous character of storytelling consists in giving an account of the happening of the singular, that is, in giving an account of what is singular in its happening" (p. 105). That *giving an account* should precede something that is "substantive in itself" seems necessary to this taking account of the singular, inasmuch as the singular here is of the order of the event. Now, when we put the eventual question "how" *before* the substantive question "who," and even before the question "*what* is this justice that's to be done?," we are not just deferring the ethical register: we may be destroying its classic shape—the shape in which an action is taken by a subject who attends to experience and circumstances, understands them, acts upon that understanding, and is thus responsible *to* circumstance and experience. In the beginning was the act, the *how*—before the subject and experience take on substance, even the substance of a name. Our tenses come into rhythm—from the how of the beginning, in the beginning, in the perfect past; to the present, when we say "Now, at this moment, I take account of the beginning, or 'I' takes account of the beginning and begins, as 'I,' and can become responsible for what 'I' does, justly, in view of reparation or restitution in the future." But this beginning that allows me, I, to begin, is also the end, the destruction of the classical ethical register: the expression *dar cuenta* also means something like "to put paid" or, as the hoary *Diccionario de la Real Academia de la Lengua* puts it, *[D]ar cuenta de algo, Dar fin de algo destruyéndolo o malgastándolo*, to end or terminate something by destroying it or using it unwisely. The last turn of Pablo Oyarzun's *Doing Justice* allows us to imagine how the narrative destruction that flows from placing the *how* of doing justice before its substance may be translated into a strange, estranged ethical register. *Darse cuenta* is the story of how one gives oneself a story before there is someone to receive it and before the story concerns anything substantive: the ethical register of the "ante-predicative." We have moved from offering a representation, an account, an allegory of justice to the much more unsettling realization that doing justice *is* allegory. What must concern us, in the wake of Pablo Oyarzun's readings of Benjamin, is the translation of justice as allegory into effective social action: the production of political subjectivities on the great avenues of Santiago, on the streets of Los Angeles, even here, always now.

Prologue

Doing Justice?

As will be seen, the three essays gathered here grew out of different occasions and different intentions. Two of them served as introductions to my translations of Walter Benjamin ("On the Concept of History" and related texts, and "The Storyteller"), while the other, the earliest of the three, was an attempt to address, in a more or less systematic way, the young Benjamin's understanding of language and translation. In principle, they might seem to share nothing but the name of Benjamin and, perhaps, some vague echo that bounces between them: nothing more, that is, than having been written on the strength of a singular experience.

Every act of reading or writing has its context, its inscription. Each one, when it tries to be thoughtful because the subject matter demands it, seeks to inscribe the context at the same time as it is inscribed by it. This happens in the resistance that the context puts up, which is precisely resistance against being inscribed and circumscribed by an act of reading or writing. It is appropriate that this resistance should be so tenacious that, in the effort to inscribe its subject matter, something comes to the surface—on the very basis of what I so casually called the context of reading and writing—that is latent in the context but overflows it or undercuts it, without limits. This is what I allude to as "a singular experience." An experience always overflows its context. And Benjamin's texts, the ones I talk about here and so many others, have this force, this tenacity, because they owe themselves to a singular radical experience, one that was thought in a radical way.

In some way, and apart from whatever intentions or ideas one may have had, apart from the expectations and distress, the sleepless nights and fatigue and the mere inertia to which one might have given in, this experience was, and is, an experience of mourning—but mourning from which the very condition of its "process" or "work" has been subtracted. Time has been taken away from it, leaving its temporality stripped of time: time, that is, and dilated time. In a sense, perhaps, interminable time is what the process or work of mourning requires. But, then, temporality remains stripped of its time, because this time has its own signature, and the dilation of which I speak is not simply time and more time—persistence that gradually gives way—but, in its beginnings, in the very first dawning of loss, a sort of sinking of time into itself. It is the sinking that we precariously name "never again." Precariously, because it is the "never again" of the *desaparecidos*, whose presence remains there, who are around, suffering in their disappearance, on the alert for an "always still," in the most lethal of conditions. But it is lethal and not mortal, because what the *desaparecidos* have been denied in their disappearance is precisely their mortality.

It is not, then, the "never again" of the phrase "so we might never again," often uttered in pain and sorrow on the streets of our devastated countries, as if to seal a promise, or sometimes pronounced from a podium, like a ritual-istic and merely conventional dictum. This "never again," therefore, is like that which resists the promise, because, in order to avoid being a practice or a gesture that fulfills a duty but remains impotent to show contrition, it must be said, uttered at the edge of the "never again." It resists, that is, from the depths of pain and from the threat that, once again, it intensifies over and over—but in a special way this time, this time above all. And the threat shows its obscene sneer while saying "always"—yes, not "always, still" but rather "always, again and again," "always, and for always."

For this very reason, there is another overflowing; not only mourning and distress get concentrated into this "never again." There is also the claim, the reclamation of justice, the demand that justice should be done. And even where pain has suffocated the word, even where the word might seem to have been cut off at its root in the throat, what this experience requires, what this silence itself enjoins without being articulated in its self-absorbed, terrified silence is that justice be done. May justice be done for the horrors and atrocities that were perpetrated, done in name of their victims. And, also, may justice be done to the very experience that asserts itself as testimony that such horrors and atrocities happened, that they lacerated and mutilated the collective body. Because if this were not the case, if this experience were obliterated together with that to which it bears witness, truth would get lost forever, a truth that requires experience and testimony, the infinite fragility of testimony. Truth and justice are not a synthesis, or they are one only in an asymptotic relationship. The demand for the truth of what has happened arises each time injustice imposes itself, and for this reason the truth, when one demands it, measures out its own distance from justice. If justice were served, if justice were done categorically and definitively, one would not require anything more from the truth, or, to put it another way, justice would finally have been done to truth.

May justice be done: what do we mean when we speak of doing justice? What does it mean to declare that justice was done? What is meant by the words "justice will be done"?[1] I suppose that, if one of us, right now, right here, were to utter one of these expressions with reference to some situation, some case, some offense, the speaker would believe that she or he knew full well what was being said, the meaning, the scope of the statement. Nevertheless, the mere thought of what one claims to do or to have done, or the thought of what one claims in a desiderative or imperative manner (the distinction is none too clear here) will be, will be done, should be or become, the thought of what will have to prevail beyond all contingencies and conditions—the mere thought of these modalities requires that knowing and the certainty of it (or at least the confidence) inevitably give way. They give way, because saying and what is said do not suffice for that which knowing and certainty say.

In the word "justice," language speaks beyond itself and beyond everything that language *can do*. *Allo agoreuei*, "it says something other," something absolutely other than all that which is capable, other from all that language can accomplish and from all that can be done. An opening occurs—language occurs— this otherness opens up with such an event, but not through it. And this opening is abysmal. With the word "justice," language does not name anything that might be made unequivocal or that could be made present as the thing it designates. Language opens itself up to such otherness, but language would not have the power to open otherness by its own means. This otherness opens itself insofar as it is not "touched" by language, insofar as it is the "beyond" of language to which the word "justice" alludes. It measures, to put it one way, the distance that separates itself from its capacity.[2] What does the word "justice" say, express, profess, or proffer? In it language speaks beyond that of which it is capable, and in this way language points toward what exceeds all human capabilities. And this is precisely the capacity of language, its power.

Nonetheless, it often happens that we know something, or rather we believe we know something. And in this belief we are certain, or we trust our ability to know what we are talking about when we say "justice," until a concrete case comes to light in which, by all appearances, the meaning that we believe we have turns problematic. Even so, faced with this case, we can be moved to speak, convinced of the truth of what we say, for example when we say "justice was done [*se hizo justicia*]."

What is said when one says "justice was done"? One hears the phrase used with reference to the most diverse situations, but it carries a charge that exceeds each one of them and all of them together, every past and future case. The absolute speaks in it in the mode of withdrawal from every particular instance in which the phrase and word might be applied. Of course, it is not possible to state, with regard to any of the imaginable cases, that "justice was done" in an absolute sense. The certainty of our putative knowledge about justice gives way. Let us consider the case of a crime involving premeditation and atrocity. The murderer, although suspected of acting as executioner, avoids even the possibility of being tried, thanks to a lack of secure evidence and unequivocal proof. He gets away with it for years. Finally, when he is captured for a lesser crime, someone manages to put the old story back together, tracing the deed back to him through a series of clues, as if by following recognizable footsteps. The criminal is sentenced to life in prison, or perhaps to the death penalty (if the laws of the country allow it). The family, even the entire society declares: "justice was done." Maybe (in the country with this legislation) family members even bear witness that justice has been carried out. But, surely, in most of these cases (or possibly in all of them) there would be no way of distinguishing with absolute clarity, and completely beyond doubt, that the "justice" that has been done has nothing to do with vengeance. In a certain way and in a certain sense, this is the essential problem of what we call "justice": the problem of its concept and of the word itself, of that which the word names and what it might name, what it would name, the problem of the bare possibility of there *being* justice. Only if, in a given case, what we call "justice" can be discerned in a constitutive way, separated out, distinguished infinitely from the primordial depths—the dark, bloody, atrocious realm of vengeance—is it possible for us *to have* justice, in the strict temporal indefiniteness of such a possession.

But this utterance involves even more. "Justice *was done*": the use of the passive voice is important here.[3] There is nothing more ambiguous than situating *justice* as the subject of the sentence. On the one hand, speaking about justice as a grammatical subject does not specify what action justice performs or has performed; it only indicates that justice prevailed. Justice "does" nothing; as a subject, it is not an agent; it can only prevail or fail, and if it fails, it does so without limit. On the other hand, the grammatical construction leaves indeterminate what or who has worked in such a way that "justice might be done"; the place reserved for an agent would appear in a phrase beginning with "by," like "justice was done by the jury," for example. As a conventional mode of expression, the passive voice in "justice was done" alludes to the agents of an action while covering them up; the allusion consists precisely in masking the identity and the traces of the person who accomplishes the action about which one states "justice has been done." This cover-up can be contemptible. Allow me to appeal to my own context, to what I earlier called "a singular experience."

In 2013—forty years after the *coup d'état* in Chile, the bombardment of the seat of government, the death of Salvador Allende, and the beginning of one of the most atrocious dictatorships in Latin American history—many things were written and said in commemoration of these fateful events. However, a glimmering promise prevailed— and I use this verb, "prevail," deliberately—in Allende's final words: "May you persevere in the knowledge that, sooner rather than later, they will open up [*abrirán*] once again the great avenues along which the free man walks, so that a better society might be built." I, too, wrote a pointed text about a doubt that had plagued me for a long while. I had felt that this statement, "the great avenues *will be opened up* [se abrirán]," was lacking the pronoun that marks the passive voice. Many written versions of Allende's words correct this statement. I listened to the speech on the radio, on that gray morning of September 11, 1973, and I have never been able to forget a single word or pause. For me, it was clear that the passage in question omitted the pronoun. At some point I must have thought (even though I wish it were not true) that the strain of the moment, provoked by a most despicable act of treason, could not fail to show up in this sort of grammatical infraction. It took me forty years to understand. The pronoun was not necessary: Allende was talking about the women and men of the *Chilean people* who "sooner rather than later ... will open up ... the great avenues" as before—as in those three short years during which those women and men had felt and known the dignity of belonging to the *Chilean people*: perhaps a phantasm, perhaps a specter that from time to time recovers its omen. The students have occupied this place, taking their protest and challenge to the streets; today it is the women of the Chilean people, the women of Chile, who fill in the air with the sound of a promissory "there will be justice." As far as the pronoun is concerned, from that disastrous day onward, the ruthless regime of the passive voice [*el régimen del "se"*] was established and spread with the profusion of dark glasses and unmarked cars, with the daily surveillance and the kidnappings and disappearances, with the places where "it was known that" or "it was said that." Also, knowledge was not sought after or it was not articulated in words; and the fact that atrocities happened was mentioned with an implicit threat. This regime spread thanks to the undaunted ferocity of the faces of conscripts sent to maintain order in the very towns and streets where they had been recruited, thanks to the heinous plundering of the Chilean state by private interests that enriched themselves through ill-gotten gains, thanks to the harsh, inept speech inflicted on us by the dictator: "in this country not a leaf moves [*no se mueve ni una hoja*] without my knowing about it."

"Justice was done [*se hizo justicia*]": upon this assertion falls the shadow of the passive voice. It is an ambiguous shadow, a secret that appears in the operation of the Spanish reflexive pronoun. "Justice was done": injured, in pain, perhaps indignant, the person who perpetrated this or that deed, taking on the guilt or whatever we may want to lay at her or his door, finally falls under the severe gaze of the administrators of justice (by which I mean the law and its agents) and suffers what is deserved: a debt incurred on account of the suffering she or he has caused. The person receives the fruit of her or his crime. The passive voice doubles back on itself. On the one hand, it covers up the executioners—subjects whom everyone can confirm anonymously without their being recognized or wanting to be recognized. In an execution, the subject of vengeance is erased qua subject of vengeance, because the execution is carried out *in the name of* (which is also supposed to mean *by the work of*) something that transcends all subjectivity, insofar as the subject is subjected to this something. It could (or should?) also be said that the subject is a subject by virtue of this subjection, of its relationship with the law. But this suggests, on the other hand, that the trace of vengeance at the origin of law has remained and is indelible. It could not be any other way, since a law that would not be applied to the singular case in its strictest and narrowest determinations would be inane. Application is what produces the law, with its case-by-case differentiations (that is, with its "in the name of," "by the rule of law"). Vengeance casts its shadow over this process of differentiation.

"There will be justice [*habrá justicia*]" is different, as is "justice will be done [*se hará justicia*]." The passive voice here, without completely eliminating the ambiguity, aims to capture an altogether different kind of situation. "There will be justice," "justice will be done," in an indeterminate temporality that corresponds to the Spanish future tense, expresses not merely what is to come but a time that represents at once all the time and pure imminence (because "justice will be done" does not state a delay or a moratorium on a debt).[4] It is, in its impersonal form, an indication (pointing in this case to the purely virtual sphere of the passive voice) that no one who presents her- or himself using the pronoun "I" may claim the faculty or the capacity to "do justice." "Justice will be done": no one will do it; *no one* is the place where that which comes imminently dwells and lingers. Benjamin gave that which comes an impersonal name, "the messianic."

Although the word *Gerechtigkeit* does not appear frequently in Benjamin's writings, I believe there is reason to state that he was a thinker of justice. He thinks of justice precisely where he thought of the messianic. He thinks of justice in his zeal for establishing an *essential* difference between law [*derecho*] and justice.[5] Of course, nowhere is the affirmation and elaboration of this difference sharper than in his early work. I have in mind, namely, "Fate and Character" and, above all, "Critique of Violence." One way or another, Benjamin attempted, in my view, to illuminate what I call here the fateful equivocity of the passive voice [*la equivocidad aciaga del "se"*] and to highlight in it all the vestiges of the demonic—this other impersonality, wrapped up as it is in vindictive, whimsical, and violent figures and poised to return at any moment, with the paraphernalia or the malicious claim of an "always, again and again." In other words, Benjamin wanted to differentiate demonic violence from a radically different kind of violence, one that is erased in the very

instant in which it is unleashed, because it has emancipatory force. This ambition has left traces on his entire
oeuvre.

In short, Benjamin thought—managed to think—in
a complex and problematic way the essential, radical,
abysmal difference between law and justice. He thought
through this difference to the point of paradox, until
a question was ignited and its gravity was felt: is it
possible to do absolutely without law in the pursuit of
justice? The suggestion of vengeance lurks in the shadows
behind this abstention from law, and this gives voice to
a warning that the relation between the two, abysmal as
the difference between them is, cannot be resolved either
a priori or on the basis of general considerations, but has
to be considered, and its resolution attempted, in every
particular case, in every particular situation. The obligation
to find a resolution in particular cases is what makes this
into an essential task, at once ethical and political.[6] Social
movements that aim at emancipation often experience this
requirement in an especially acute way.

Without omitting or forgetting the key dispute that
Benjamin invokes in the writings of his youth—namely the
recusal without appeal from the question of right and the
law [el derecho y la ley], which, in all its difficulty, pays
homage to the truth of anarchy as an asymptotic relation
in which truth and justice would have to find themselves—
I would like to refer to three other fundamental modes of
justice: the slight rectification that the messianic brings;
humor; and quotation. One way or another, the physi-
ognomy of these three motifs is revealed, I believe, in the
essays that follow. In these motifs we can hear the rever-
berations of "justice will be done," "there will be justice,"
"justice will prevail."

But "justice has been done" will not resound in them,
I would insist, because, in accordance with a gesture with
Kantian roots, we would never be able to *know* whether
justice has been done in an effective and emphatic way.

(I already mentioned vengeance as a kind of shadow that can be cast by what takes itself to be justice fulfilled according to the law; and this complicates the problem of the difference between vengeance and justice.) It is only appropriate, perhaps, that the saying "justice will be done" should be a call that can only maintain itself in its own uncertainty, as a promise and a commitment. A call, because what announces itself in its demand is a barely audible effect of the passive voice: silent, or rather quiet and inapparent work, which consists in correcting things slightly or in being faithful to the desire that nothing should get lost, precisely on account of this slight correction.[7]

The word *Entstellung*—"distortion," "displacement," "dislocation"—bears a very specific weight in some of Benjamin's texts, particularly the ones that discuss Kafka. Everything in Kafka's work, existence itself, is distorted: the *Entstellung des Daseins* ("distortion of existence") is "the sole topic of his work" (GS II.2 678, SW II 496). One of the emblems of distortion—one might say, in truth, its archetype—is the little hunchback [*das bucklichte Männlein*] that peers out of childish fantasies and insidiously provokes forgetting, lapses of attention, and carelessness, thereby causing slight blunders to trigger catastrophic effects (WN XI.1 488–490). We can imagine what makes up a world plagued by this catastrophe, understood as a generalized imbalance: it is, in Benjamin's words, Kafka's universe; and it is also our world, which a sharpened sensibility cannot help but perceive and experience in "deer-like" fright. Nonetheless the hunchback, as an emissary of forgetting—and this forgetting always "affects the possibility of redemption" (GS II.2 432; SW II 811, modified)—has for this very reason a special relationship with redemption. "This little man," says Kafka, "is at home in distorted life; he will disappear with the coming of the Messiah, who (a great rabbi once said) does not want to change the world by violence but will merely make a slight adjustment to it [*nur um ein Geringes zurechtstellen*]" (GS II.2 432, SW II 811, modified). This little change that changes everything is something that happens to distortion itself: "distortion will suppress itself [*wird sich selber aufheben*], opening the path to redemption" (GS II.3 1201). This paradoxical operation, which dislocates distortion, which displaces every single blunder and deformity and reconfigures them, which corrects them and fixes only the necessary amount, this imbalance in the general imbalance, the messianic counter-*Entstellung*, brings with it the adjustment, justice; and it brings it *immediately*, in the time of a moment of suspension, in the "there will be [*habrá*]" (and in the "they will open [*abrirán*]") of a promise and commitment.

If I may understand Benjamin in this way, this is the abrupt separation between the demonic and the messianic passive voice, both marked by the reflexive pronoun *se* in Spanish.

Another way to put the zeal of this promise and commitment to work pertains to language, "the language of man."[8] And, to tell the truth, it would not be possible to say that it is different; it is the same. In a certain way, everything happens in language, as long as it is understood that language is something more than itself, that it always goes beyond its own capacities, that its greatest power is precisely its impotence, which is demonstrated in the place where the word bows down to the name and leaves it intact.

The power of human language verges on complete impotence in the very moment in which it reigns supreme, precisely because it exceeds itself by saying—that is, by pointing toward—that which exceeds it absolutely. It is fitting that this should happen in at least two different modalities. The first is humor. This is what happens with Hebel, who measures according to the correct measures, "namely, with the measure of humor, that is, with applied justice." He measures his creatures with humor, assessing with its help their ability to enliven him through their untarnished sense of humanity. As for those who frustrate him, woe be to them! "Hebel was one of the great moralists of all times. His morality is the continuation of storytelling with other means, his humor is execution without judgement: applied justice, which measures them by a standard that is completely different from all the others. Not for nothing was the *Treasure Chest* one of Kafka's favorite books" (GS II.2 628).[9] There is humor in the little hunchback, and there is humor and justice in the slight rectification that the world requires.

Hence humor is important. In "Three Books of Today," a commentary on the work of Viktor Shklovski, Alfred Polgar, and Julien Benda, Benjamin says that the origin of Polgar's art "resides in justice, in a justice that is all the more melancholy the farther it lies from all fanaticism. If the philosophy of art were less smothered in aesthetic chatter than it has been for the last fifty years, we could count more, certainly, on this simple and important fact being understood: that all humor has its origin in justice. But, certainly, in a justice that considers not human beings but rather things to be important. Thus, instead of appearing in character or action, the ethical order would appear in a just, successful constitution of the world, or rather in the no less decisive structure of the singular case, the accident" (WN 13.1 118–119). It would make sense to think that this displacement of the human in favor of things might be precisely an exemption from the ethical— for which, by a well-established custom, we have recourse to ourselves, to what we say we are and what we feel we are. Thus it does not seem possible to speak of justice outside the sphere of things that correspond to the human, except in old maxims such as Anaximander's saying. But this is precisely the point: justice does not concern exclusively the human being, nor is the human the holder of the corresponding right [*derecho*]. In a "successful constitution of the world," *everything* has a right: the right to justice. The issue here is doing justice to the creature, whatever its ontological signature might be: doing justice in its singularity. Humor always sympathizes with what is small. It is the insignia of humor. And it is another name for the singular.

In humor the slight correction might occur in miniature.

The other variation of justice in language is the quotation. While Hebel makes humor the center of attention and nourishes the human side of the Enlightenment, Karl Kraus uses the quotation as a righteous weapon, a firearm whose caliber is measured by the entirety of language. Kraus's passion and satirical furor lie millions of miles away from Hebel's domestic bonhomie. It makes language the space and the place of honor for a juridical procedure in which the law is applied without consideration for the punitive faculty. But this same proceeding (which consists in a processing) works against the law [*derecho*], which clearly is demanded: "For this is the last official act of this zealot: to place the legal system itself under accusation ... Kraus accuses the law [*das Recht / el derecho*] in its substance, not in its effect. His charge: high treason of the law [*des Rechtes / del derecho*] against justice" (GS II.1 349, SW II 444). The principle of this essential conclusion is the conviction that "justice and language remain founded in each other" (GS II.1 349, SW II 444). Benjamin can be recognized in the appeal to this principle, which would organize Kraus's practice of citation: "To worship the image of divine justice in language—even in the German language—this is the genuinely Jewish *salto mortale* by which he tries to break the spell of the demon" (GS II.1 349, SW II 444).

The operation carried out by a quotation, "Kraus's basic polemical procedure," is therefore (decidedly) what gives an account of that conviction and of this image. It is a matter of naming: "To quote a word is to call it by its name" (GS II.1 362, SW II 453). For the same reason, quotability, if this is an appropriate word, has its limits;

not everything can be quoted, nor is everything worthy of being quoted. According to Benjamin, Kraus has gotten maximum yield from the quotation: he has made even magazines quotable. Without a doubt, quotation can be exercised in a different way. In a context that is not worthy of being quoted, it can act with punitive efficacy. And it can also rescue the word from the night in which it is lethargically trapped. "In the quotation that both saves and punishes, language proves the matrix of justice" (GS II.1 363, SW II 454).

Quotation calls the word by its name, and in this way calls it back to its origin, back to the name. Origin and destruction: this simultaneous accreditation offers language credentials regarding its origin and its destruction, reaching consummation in the complete overlapping of the two. Thus Benjamin defines an essential aspect of his understanding of both quotation and its use—and, along with it, an essential aspect of his understanding of justice. In particular, justice is not possible without a destructive moment. This very trait also characterizes the operation of humor as applied justice and occupies its vertiginous core of messianic counterdistortion. The indicator of that destructive moment is immediacy: *justice is destructive because it is immediate*. This is because it is pure mediacy, deprived of all ulterior and exterior ends, realized and actualized in itself, as in "Critique of Violence." To justice belongs the immediacy of a *now* that is nothing but the imminence (the coming now and as such, the present moment) of the justice that will be, that will be done. A justice that restores to everything and every creature that part of memory that distortion had removed and condemned to the dregs of forgetting. This is the justice of the chronicler, "who provides details of events without distinguishing between great ones and small ones, (and) takes into account the truth that nothing that ever happened can be considered lost to history." In their patient and scrupulous labor, chroniclers conspire, whether they know it or not, on behalf of redemption: "only a redeemed humanity is concerned with its past. This means: only for a redeemed humanity has the past become quotable in every one of its moments. Each one of its lived instants is converted into a *citation à l'ordre du jour* ["quotation of the day"], a day that is precisely that of Judgement Day" (WN XIX 31).

Justice is not, nor can it be, a deed, an order, an agreement, a reckoning; it is nothing that can be done or found *in the world.* In a fragment titled "Notizen zu einer Arbeit über die Kategorie der Gerechtigkeit" ["Notes on a Study on the Category of Justice"] that is not included in Tiedemann and Schweppenhäuser's edition of *Gesammelte Schriften,* a fragment written in 1916 and kept by Gershom Scholem, Benjamin defines justice as "the striving to turn the world into the highest good [*Gerechtigkeit ist das Streben, die Welt zum höchsten Gut zu machen*]."[10] "Effort" names that which concerns responsibility for the world we share. This effort, which takes aim at the world itself, neither concedes nor confirms the world as it is. If justice is this effort or is indissociably linked to it, present in it, justice can only be a state of the world (*ein Zustand der Welt*) in which the world is no longer merely given and those who take responsibility are no longer subjects of right or subjects *tout court*: they are existents. "Justice appears not to be based upon the good will of the subject, but forms the state of the world. Justice refers to the ethical category of the existing, virtue the ethical category of the demanded."[11]

Doing justice? Justice cannot be done, unless doing justice consists in the exertion devoted to doing justice, even in cases—also and perhaps above all in cases—in which this exertion might cost an existent his or her life. The invocation "justice will be done" resounds in that very place. In that very place, this call for justice points in a direction that radically outstrips the world as what is given and absolutely surpasses everything that a subject *can do.* "Justice will be done" names the secret force that awakens responsibility, that encourages the effort. Justice will *be* done [*Se hará justicia*].

In the end, perhaps the ear that endeavored to hear the *se* of the passive in Allende's promise did not err completely. In this promise, "they will open the great avenues," the women and the men, the workers of Chile, summoned by the promise—as they were and as they will have been, as existents—will be secretly assisted by a passivity without identity or name, inaudible, forever persistent, which is nothing but a threshold that, perhaps, gives or would give way to the world as the supreme good, as *another* world. But the passage, and that world, insist and persist only in the promise, in the time of the promise, a promise that measures time.

There will be justice. They will open up the great avenues.

I live—we live—on a promise.

1

On Benjamin's Concept
of Translation

Preamble

Even if Walter Benjamin's thought had not already capti-
vated us in its own right—with its multiple tensions,
the fragility of its insights, its dizzying paradoxes—our
interest in his concept of translation would still be well
justified. In recent years, translation has risen to the rank
of a philosophical problem of the highest order.

More or less unanimously, previous philosophers never
felt the need to explicitly develop a conception of translation, or even to address it as a theme or as a matter
worthy of consideration. The fields of rhetoric, textual
scholarship, and theological hermeneutics have turned
their attention to translation in ways that are not restricted
to problems of practice. For philosophy, however, during
the centuries of what we commonly call the "tradition,"
translation has referred, above all and almost exclusively,
to an activity or a resource, not to a structure or an
essence. It has addressed the eminently technical question
of the nature of language and multiplicity of languages,
signifiers remaining subservient to the strict transcendental

leveling effect of the signified. And, while this tradition continues to be surreptitiously woven with the threads of an incessant translativity, philosophical meaning has established a relationship with language (and languages) that is as necessary as it is supposed to be natural.[1]

It is precisely the naturalness of the relationship between philosophy and language (and languages) that has come to be interrogated and raised to the rank of an essential and unavoidable question in contemporary thought. In this respect, the recent privilege accorded to the problem of translation contributes to what we might call the "linguistic totalization" of the horizon of philosophical questions that cuts across, as it were, the prevailing currents in philosophy today.

But this privilege is not simply a particular case of the concern for genre. It reveals an aspect of this concern that appears only in a phase that might deserve to be called "radical." In effect, the tendency specific to this totalization consists in referring all ontological questions (of being, existence, and reality) back to language. This tendency reaches its culmination—or in any case an acute phase—when, beyond the isomorphism between language and "what is," language itself comes to be conceived of consistently as process and as praxis, as performance and as event, all of them *open*, because of the impossibility of their being grounded in referential objectivity or in mental interiority. In this process, the ontological, and what we could call being itself, would appear accommodated and dispersed in the play of performances, of instances of referral or interpretation.

From this angle, translation offers itself as the most general concept available that can give an account of all the intra- and interlinguistic performances *as* performances. What we could legitimately characterize as the philosophical "pre-concept" of translation (which is also, essentially, a prejudice or pre-judgement and already comes into focus in ancient Greece) confirms, in its "practical" inflection, this performative character. In spite of all the rectifications it has undergone, the concept of communication retains its subservience to objectivist or intersubjectivist suppositions (whether at an empirical or at a transcendental level). By contrast, the first philosophical inscription of translation, in rhetoric, defines it as a type of linguistic performance, a process of setting to work a *lexis* ["discourse"] that is different from semantics and from *hupokrisis* ["delivery"], a *lexis* understood as an unlimited system of displacements.[2] If translation has been able to occupy the scene of theoretical reflection as it does today, this is because it could be conceived of in its own right, as an internal equivalent to language and languages, as the language in all languages, and as a paradigm for the process—and death—of being in language and in languages. In fact, if we may argue that onto*logy* reveals itself as the epitome or pinnacle of the western project of knowing, we could assume that this absorption or complete dehiscence of being in language has been prescribed from the start according to a certain interpretation of the *logos* and in agreement with a certain (unlimited) exposure of being to the play of interpretation, of *hermēneia*.

If we attempt to situate Benjamin within this context—which I immediately confess to having sketched out in a clumsy and merely indicative way—what might he require us to say about how his thinking reckoned with the correspondence between language and being? Does Benjamin accommodate being into language, perhaps in translation, in the relationship that translation also bears, as the intangible does, to the original (text, being)?

I

Before we allow a precipitous answer to this question, it is worth considering the unprecedented balance maintained between two statements from an early essay from 1916, which itself is unprecedented and, it seems to me, uncontrollable: "*Über Sprache überhaupt und über die Sprache des Menschen*," "On Language as Such and on the Language of Man."

The spiritual being [*das geistige Wesen*] of a thing consists precisely in its language—this view, taken as a hypothesis, is the great abyss into which all linguistic theory threatens to fall. (GS II.1 141; SW I 63, modified)

Language is thus [*dann*] the spiritual being of things. (GS II.1, 145; SW I 66, modified)

I have no intention of commenting immediately upon the matter that is brought into a state of tension in these assertions. That requires patient and detailed attention to the contexts in which they are offered, the turns of argument, and the leaps outside the reasoning that connects them. By placing them in a relation of contiguity that, if perhaps excessive, is also implicit in the text and in the work (or play) of its incommensurable hiatuses, I would merely like to call attention to the flagrant friction between the two, which in a certain sense is irreducible. I believe that this gives us a quick warning about the complexity of Benjamin's answer to the question I have posed, a complexity that threatens to submerge that answer in an abyss. In a sense, Benjamin answers "yes" and "no" *at the same time*, and it would not be pertinent to see in this a refusal to reply. Thus the question reveals itself as an abyss. Being (spiritual being or essence, according to the essay's lexicon)—being and language are *not* the same, except on a hypothesis that is, like the seduction (*Versuchung*) of the beginning, the abyss of philosophizing. This precaution, this warning and shield, this self-protection of the beginning should be stipulated, of course, at the beginning. But being and language *are* the same: they are both said, or rather they both speak *as* the same thing; spiritual being and linguistic being coincide. They share an identity in the uncontainable push of an inference (*dann*) and of a time of inference (a time and a *place*, the center, not the beginning; see GS II.1 141, SW I 63) that does not admit logic or control or formal administration of what is thought, because it is nothing but the impulse to form, or to the medium, before any content.

In the first place, what links the two assertions is the condition that weighs on the first: "and to survive suspended precisely over this abyss is its task" (GS II.1 141, SW I 63). Benjamin speaks here of the task of the theory of language, of its *Aufgabe*: I will have opportunity to raise the question of this term when I address the translator's task, which simultaneously implies, as we will see, a mission—an imposition—and a renunciation. It is an abysmal task, in any case: above this abyss—the abyss of philosophical activity,[3] an abyss that is constitutive of all thought that aims at the foundations but that, constitutively, has to despair of the abyss—the theory of language must maintain itself, suspended. We can already predict that this suspension is language itself, hanging over a foundation that is lacking, that it lacks insofar as it cannot make it present to itself—and hanging like a swaying bridge between two cliffs—being, language, the being of being and the being of language: theory of language has tended to think of language as a bridge beyond all appearances and wills and before what the "merely" figurative use of the term would be, as a passage between two shores that are distant and cannot be brought closer, as a means of navigation or travel, a vehicle (for meaning), a metaphor, a translation.

If this persistence over the abyss offers the key to Benjamin's proposition at the same time as it conceals it, because we cannot know the movement of its "survival" ahead of time, the phrase "being and language are the same" should be true on *a certain reading* that pertains to it. But the *production* of this reading is necessary in order to *install* that truth. And the production of this reading demands that we carry out the *critique* of another reading, one that reveals itself as the dominant one. This other reading is what Benjamin calls the "bourgeois conception of language" (GS II.1 144, SW I 65), which makes language only a mediation, which reduces the word to a sign and in the sign recognizes the abstract form of the commodity. Being and language are certainly identified here to the extent that they are leveled out and reduced to exchange value and to universal equivalence: in this way communication is interpreted—and thus it is experienced—as an exchange of objects between human beings, exactly as some ironic anti-utopia of language would want to represent it.[4] The interchangeability of objects, which also includes the addressees, extends into an interchangeability of names, their fundamental insignificance. This complete and universal capacity for permutations resolves being and language in the identity of a convention. The "bourgeois conception of language" is what Benjamin conceived of, in the last instance, as the historically transformed truth of the conventionalist thesis.

The critique to which I alluded above is based on this thesis. In the secular debate around the origin and nature of language, Benjamin's meditation, by virtue of its tenacious resistance to the conversion of the word into a sign and to the ellipsis of the name, preemptively inscribes itself into the naturalist heritage, although one should pay attention to the mode of this inscription, which is by no means simple, since it bears the labyrinthine mark of duplicity (a "yes," a "no") and of a suspension over the abyss.

Another text, this time years away from the youthful first one, speaks eloquently of the elective affinity: "Of the Mimetic Faculty" (*"Über das mimetische Vermögen,"* GS II.1 210–213, SW II 720–722). This is the second sketch of a theme that intensely preoccupied Benjamin in 1933.[5] Benjamin argues here that the mimetic faculty—that of perception and production of similarities and analogies, where we find an echo of the Aristotelian theme of the metaphorical talent as well as Baudelaire's motif of *correspondances*—is characteristic of human beings because they excel in it.[6] In addition, the mimetic faculty has a history: the history of its transformation. The meaning of this transformation consists in the unfolding of "immaterial similarity." Beyond the magical suppositions that were first able to illuminate it in human experience, and also beyond the apparent benumbing of the aptitude to apprehend it, the field, the "canon" in which the domain of similarity comes to prevail for us, is in language and in languages.

But to give satisfaction to the injunction that this (hidden) reign involves, it is necessary to understand in depth the efficacy of the mimetic faculty in the development of language, without becoming paralysed in the usual resources of the naturalism of onomatopoeia, which relies on sensible similarities. What we should do, rather, is develop the "program" that the onomatopoeic conception of language carries implicitly within itself. In this way the reformulation of the thesis of mimetism in the formation of language and of languages requires the concept of immaterial similarity, represented as a concentric orbiting of words from various languages on the basis of their allusion to a single meaning—an allusion to the same that opens between them the intangible dimension of a virtual kinship: similarity.[7]

Benjamin does not think of the similarity in which this concentricity consists in terms of signification. The very word by which he names it, *Ähnlichkeit*, is of a purely allusive rather than signifying nature. It points to subtle links that have the consistency of something atmospheric, the feel of relationships forged by marriage, the efficacy of presentiment. They are not reducible to the iron rails of signification. It might be said that Benjamin essentially decided to invert the hierarchical relationship between signification (*logos*) and similarity (*mimēsis*). He did not intend to abolish the first, but ultimately to remove it from the arbitrariness of the link that connects sign and object, so as to reserve it as the promise of languages. But this, no doubt, should carry with it an essential modification, a reinterpretation of *logos* itself. Certainly the "semiotic side" of language—customarily apprehended under the condition of that arbitrariness—is determined as a support, a substructure, and a brace—upon which, "in the manner of lightning," similarity strikes: the reference to the central meaning. Looked at from the less apparent perspective of how the semiotic serves the mimetic, "language may be seen as the highest level of mimetic behavior and the most complete archive of nonsensual similarity" (GS II.1 213, SW II 722).

For the same reason, even more essential than that inversion is the way the referential connection surpasses signification through hint (*Ahnung*). As I see it, this defines in a decisive manner something we could call the crux of Benjamin's work: something that, in any case, is not—as I already said about the purpose of inversion—a putative abandonment of the semantic space but an unrestricted *temporalization* of signification. This is what I was pointing out by speaking of a reinterpretation of *logos*, which will no longer admit the present as its exemplary and fundamental matrix but will maintain it distended between memory and promise, between evocation and announcement, between call and echo.

The fragment that we are discussing does not clarify what the *principle* of non-sensible similarities might be or how we might think it. It does not explain "what is signified" "as" the signifying (that is, evocative) "center" (*das Bedeutete ... als Mittelpunkt*) when multiple words from multiple languages say "the same" (*das Gleiche*). Furthermore, we could perhaps conjecture that this text's *task* renounces this clarification, that is, it only arouses the idea of central signification as an essential fugacity (*sie huscht vorbei*, "it scurries past," says Benjamin of similarity), the fleeting quality of the semiotic brushing lightly against the mimetic, a pure tangent. Thus we can ascertain this same meaning in the mimetic references of language, which themselves are no more than fleeting and whose peculiar play, the wake they leave in their flight, also fails to receive clarification.

But this does not mean, as one might too quickly assume, handing the theory of language over to random exploitation by mystical excess. It feeds into what we might describe as a *schwärmerisch* [wishful] variant of naturalism. In the end, it can bear no more fruit than a perfect (and, for this reason, equally ideological) inversion of conventionalism and mercantilism of the sign: it also premeditates the identity between language and being, except that it does not disperse it in the publicity of relationships of unlimited permutations that can be capitalized in economic, social, and political ways. Instead, it reserves this identity for the privacy of a vision (which can also be very lucrative). In this respect, we should follow carefully the arguments of the text, as it avoids dissipating the specificity of linguistics (a specificity that gets lost in other conceptions) and sets about creating a place for it once and for all. I said before, with a term that was not altogether propitious, that the hierarchy between *logos* and *mimēsis* gets inverted here, but the axis of this inversion can be located in the signifying relationship. In other words, it is not a matter of covering the essence of language with a new doctrinal formulation but of producing a displacement in this essence itself that would push it out of its prevailing, controlled equilibrium. Signification and, in general, semiosis, as the basic mechanism of language, is separated from sense and interpreted in its core, or rather in accordance with that which is its meaning itself, to the extent that it is mimetic. (And, let me say this in advance, without proof: in this notion, already modified with respect to its classical, naturalist predecessors, the concept of translation is announced.) The essential relation of language and languages is not, then, one that signs establish among themselves, on the basis of some "semantic nexus" (*Sinnzusammenhang*), but one that, like an asymptote, opens up and stretches out from each word and from each phrase toward its meaning.

The "argumentative movement" of this fragment should nonetheless be gleaned from the movement of the first essay that I cited. In the fragment, language has been allowed to emerge as the "highest level" of the natural history of the mimetic faculty, in such a way that the movement—whose sense is deposited in the mimetic concentration of names around a purely immaterial meaning—proceeded *from language to being*. By contrast, the essay expressly extends the notion of language to the whole of nature, the totality of what is, but at the same time it secures the notion of spiritual essence as its principal category, in the same place where the other text reserves the central meaning. It shows a movement *from being toward language*. Where both movements cross, as the quick and fleeting friction between them, we note an interminable resistance: the refusal to identify language and being *any further*, that is, to identify them without distinguishing between the two readings of the phrase that says "being and language are the same." Let us recall that all this was a matter of rendering the second reading, the *other* reading, comprehensible and practicable.

Benjamin's use of the concept of communication (*Mitteilung*) belongs to the circuit of this other reading. Everything communicates, namely its content, its spiritual being, and in this way it participates (*teilhat*) in language in a certain way and to a certain degree (see GS II.1 140–141, SW I 62–63). The appeal to a concept that sounds so close to conventional notions might seem strange, but the transformation of the concept of communication follows precisely from this idea that everything communicates its spiritual essence (its being) and removes it from what we might call its "informativist" component and from the supposition that in communication *something* is communicated (see GS II.1 141, SW I 62–63). This leads to an approximation of the notions of communication and expression that makes them inseparable in Benjamin's analysis and that reaches its peak in the concept of revelation, in which the two fuse. On account of this new interpretation, Benjamin suppresses the consideration of language as mere mediation: he conceives of it now as an element. This is the crucial distinction between "through" and "in": "It is fundamental to know that this spiritual being communicates itself *in* (*in*) language and not *through* (*durch*) language" (GS II.1 142; SW I 63, modified). Precisely this "through" dominates the conventional understanding of communication, whose desideratum is a *transparency* of language, assumed, aspired to as the *ideal* of language, as an ideal language (or, if you will, as language without mother tongue [*lenguaje sin lengua*]). Diversely, the appropriate image for what is involved in the "in" would be language as a crystal, that is, as the precipitate of the spiritual content in a form, the form of a recipient (later we will discuss the metaphor of the vessel)—which is precisely the communicable part of this content and, as far as communicability goes, the whole content. And the crystal does not refer to ideality but to purity, not to a language without mother tongue but to a *pure* mother tongue.[8] But let us not get ahead of ourselves.

The communication of being in language, and not through itself, marks being's irreducibility to language.[9] The hardness or the resistance of what is crystalline about the "in": only in communicability can being and linguistic being be identified. "Spiritual being is identical with linguistic being only *insofar as* it is *capable of* communication. What is communicable in a spiritual being is its linguistic being. Language therefore communicates the particular linguistic being of things, but their spiritual

being only insofar as it is *capable of* being communicated"
(GS II.1 142; SW I 63, modified).

But language does not happen unexpectedly [*no le
sobreviene*] to being, from the outside, as if it were
possible to locate it in an exterior of this sudden event
[*sobre-venimiento*]. Being and language are identical only
to the extent that we consider the communicable aspect of
a being; but in any case its communicability is necessary to
being. We could in fact conjecture that this necessity is the
strict meaning that ought to be attributed to Benjamin's
concept of the spiritual (*geistig*) in this context, and this is
the very necessity that imposes the appeal to this concept
in the text.

"Language communicates the linguistic being of things"
(GS II.1 142, SW I 63): it communicates being as linguistic
being. But the linguistic being of a thing is its particular
language. Thus language (the particular language) communicates with itself. This accomplishes two things: the
reticence of being in language, the impossibility of accom-
modating it in immanent linguistic relations; and at the
same time the specificity of language as the eloquence of
the tongue that transmits itself, that—to use a particularly
appropriate term—is its own *message*. I have already
said that this specificity could not be understood as
mediation but is rather medium, element. Thought of
from outside itself, it requires us to take one step further:
the mediateness of language—which, in a radical sense,
is something other than mediation—is determined as its
immediacy. This is the immediacy of being in linguistic
being and the immediacy of linguistic being as a particular
language. *In* itself, language communicates something
other, being: the essence of the message is allegory (*allo
agoreuō*, "I say something else").[10]

The human is, for the time being, an instance of the
universal assertion "the linguistic being of a thing is its
particular language." Nonetheless, her or his language
consists in the word—that is, essentially, in the name. "The

human therefore communicates her or his own spiritual being (insofar as it is communicable) by *naming* all other things. ... *It is therefore the linguistic being of the human to name things*" (GS II.1 143, SW I 64, modified). This means that the human communicates her or his being in the name. With the determination of this instance, Benjamin reaches the peak of his polemic with conventionalism: the task proposed here has the basic character of a *rescue*, in other words it is a task of rescuing the name in the word as that which the bourgeois conception of language buries in the sign. But surely it would be pointless to seize upon this instance, the name, in a merely nominal way (and it would be easy to confuse Benjamin's idea with traditional theories of naming),[11] without taking into account the instance of that constitutive alterity that, as I recently said, determines the being of language without pausing to reflect on how what it does to the name is other and the other, without pausing to reflect that the name is always a name of an other for an other. The name is heterology, not only because in it something other (a being) might be named, said, or communicated but also because, if the name is not a mere sheath for meaning but the topos of communication, then all names always refer to (or name) another name. *The particular language that names is language par excellence* [por antonomasia].[12] Antonomasia—a rhetorical figure categorized as a synecdoche that consists of substituting an appellative for the proper name (or vice versa)—would be the most appropriate designation for this peculiar movement. That human languages should consist of names is what determines the human as the quintessential communicant—the one whose *being* is referred to and in the name, whose being grows (germinates and flowers) in the name—a purely transitive place where the other is turned toward the other. As antonomasia, the name is a version. And translation plays a role here—once again.

But if the human is the quintessential communicant, then her or his spiritual being itself is language tout court. This

is not limited to a simple reiteration of the philosopheme
that defines the human as *zōon logon echon* ["animal
endowed with reason"]. Language, being centered on the
name, does not constitute a sameness of inalienable being,
or a sheath, as no more than a vocation of otherness,
which is—not only with respect to otherness, but itself
as a vocation, as we will see shortly—the essence of the
name. Once human beings are constituted in this way,
things communicate their being to us to the extent that the
latter are communicable; they communicate their linguistic
being and we communicate their being ... to God. Human
beings name things, we name them and address them by
name, and we ourselves are called *in* our being by name
to the extent that we express ourselves in names. This is
what Benjamin characterizes as the "essential law," that is,
the "law of the essence" (*Wesensgesetz*) of language: "to
express oneself (*sich selbst aussprechen*) and to address
everything else (*alles andere ansprechen*) amounts to the
same thing (*dasselbe*)" (GS II.1 145, SW I 65). I think that
this is a decisive point and I would even like to venture to
see in it the center of the "center" in the theory of language
that Benjamin assembles and disassembles, insofar as that
he invokes this third term, the law (*la ley*), as that which
relates one to the other in the same copula, being and
language. Hence one could say that the law of essence (of
Wesen, that is, of being) is at the same time the essence
of law: according to it, law is that to which being itself is
called, from out of itself. Or rather, more precisely, being
is being called, but law is the call itself. Law and being,
certainly irreducible to each other, communicate (with
each other) in the call, and this communication is precisely
what we call language and languages. They communicate
in the name, and the call is the being of the human being;
the being of the human being is therefore to be called to
account by the law.[13]
    The foregoing considerations can help us understand
the two strange themes whose intertwining in Benjamin's

meditation might go completely unnoticed. The first is that the name is language [*lenguaje*] strictly speaking, the only language [*lengua*], *die Sprache schlechthin*, given that in it being is called to be linguistic. The name is the criterion, if I may put it this way, according to which the spiritual being conforms itself to linguistic being. The second theme is that the name, qua pure call, says nothing, neither outside the call nor inside the call: *"there is no such thing as a content* (Inhalt) *of a particular language"* (GS II.1 145, SW I 66). This (hypo)thesis is decisive for the definition, which I offered earlier, of language as message, as missive.

We can consider both themes to be summed up in the appeal to the medial as the substance of language: with it Benjamin attempts to think communicability (*Mitteilbarkeit*) and immediacy (*Unmittelbarkeit*) at the same time, and this means thinking the immediacy of communicability and conceiving of communicability as immediacy. It is an absolute brush with mysticism, yet only a brush. Benjamin speaks instead of "magic." This concept—which will figure in the brief text "On the Mimetic Faculty"—inherits the sense of *mimēsis*. "Magic" indicates the availability of a transgeneric passage; it alludes to contagion as a kind of regression to—and, simultaneously, an overcoming of—the rigidity of logic. The outcome is a mimetic conception of communication. As a result, *mitteilen*, communication or sharing, has here the meaning of uninterrupted continuity, which expresses itself in a doctrinal way in the notion of "degrees of being" (spiritual, linguistic). At the end of the essay, where he recapitulates his ideas, Benjamin says: "The uninterrupted flow of this communication [of the spiritual being of each thing] runs through the whole of nature, from the lowest forms of existence to man and from man to God" (GS II.1 157, SW I 74). Nevertheless, this uninterrupted continuity is constituted in an integral way by interruptions: its moments are so many languages, each one irreducible to the others because there does not exist in any of them a content from which they could be derived, explained. They are their own content: "The language of nature is comparable to a secret password that each sentry hands down to the next in her or his own language, but the meaning of the password is the sentry's language itself" (GS II.1 157, SW I 74).

The notion of this uninterrupted continuity of interruptions responds to Benjamin's interest in carrying to its furthest consequences what he himself—in the fragment from which I took my point of departure—called the "program" of the mimetic (or onomatopoeic) conception. This interest is peculiar in that it resists every tendency in that conception to base itself merely on imitation, copying, or "reflection." And this means two things at once. He is opposed to a material (*inhaltlich*, centered on the content) interpretation of similarity, one that reduces the meaning of similarity to what we might call quantitative equalization or, if you will, mercantile equivalence: the administration of the continuity of similarity on the basis of the circulation of "things that are alike." At the same time, he rejects the control of relations of similarity by reference to a generic framework, from which similarity can only be understood as homogeneity. It is completely relevant to recall here the absolutely unique efficacy that Benjamin wants to see deposited in *Ähnlichkeit*: the efficacy of presentiment and kinship, of the analogical, and of that which—à la Wittgenstein—we could appeal to as "family resemblance" and, even more decisively, as the power, allusive and elusive, of allegory. (Allusive and elusive because allusion *takes care of*—it watches over, guards, and preserves—the "flight," the absence of what is elusive, and thus is its *name*.)[14]

So it is precisely with this power in view[15] that the decisive meaning of translation is determined. To put it another way, the concept of translation is truly suitable for giving an account of the power of allegory, since it allows one to think of similarity as a process of transformation. *Kontinuum von Verwandlungen* ["continuum of transformations"] is the phrase that Benjamin uses to determine the space in which the mobility of translation takes place. Translation is "the transporting (*Überführung*) of one particular language into another through a continuum of transformations" (GS II.1 151, SW I 70, modified). The perfectly paradoxical idea of this continuum can be found at the innermost core of Benjamin's approach to the conception of language. To this extent, the necessity of "grounding the concept of translation at the deepest level of linguistic theory" (GS II.1 151, SW I 69), as Benjamin puts it, can be considered one of the most decisive motifs of his essay. And we have already seen that this continuity cannot be understood in the sense of homogeneity: all homogeneity is fractured ahead of time by the constitutive difference between being and language, between spiritual and linguistic being, and, within the latter, between muteness and revelation. Homogeneity is fractured, but at the same time the instances I have mentioned remain linked through a secret and inviolable alliance. How might we think and summarize this double determination? I think one could postulate the affirmation of an *infinitesimal difference* as the essential mobility of the continuum. This same difference, as I will try to show, will take on a decisive meaning in the essay on the task of the translator, in agreement with the motif of the intangible and the tangent as subtle and fleeting (con)tact. It may be argued, on the basis of an evocation in the 1933 text devoted to the mimetic faculty, that this difference can be conceived of as the idea (the image) that the continuum is traversed by the lightning bolt of similarity, in the form or sign of a consummation. In this momentary flash, languages acquire their essential kinship in reference, that is, in the salvation of difference as difference. Reference extends backwards from languages themselves and from everything that is and can be communicated to God's pure word, which resides in itself.

II

In Benjamin's 1916 essay "On Language," translation is above all from the language of things into the particular language spoken by a human being, as a translation of the mute. For nature is mute and therefore sorrowful, since it suffers in mourning for the lack of *Sprache* and suffers infinitely, because all human languages, in their fallenness, are at fault. Thus translation is a translation of the mute to the sonorous and from that which lacks a name (*das Namenlose*) to the named. "It is therefore the translation of an imperfect language into a more perfect one, and cannot but add something to it, namely knowledge" (GS II.1 151, SW I 70). But this very transition from the imperfect to the perfect can be predicated on the relationship between the multiple languages of human beings (among which one could count Adam's language) and the divine word, whose full power is creation. For this reason, from that specific meaning one can come to establish the general meaning with which the essay concludes: "All higher language is a translation of lower ones, until in ultimate clarity the [untranslatable] word of God unfolds, which is the unity of this movement made up of language" (GS II.1 157, SW I 74).

One might think that "The Task of the Translator," written in 1923, carries with it a restriction of the open perspective of the earlier essay. In effect, in tune with this text's fate of serving as preface to Benjamin's version of Baudelaire's *Tableaux parisiens*, Benjamin gives priority to the work of poetry at the heart of the language of names and of the relationship between the multiple languages of human beings. But we should take into account the peculiarity of the movement of Benjamin's argument, if we can still apply this name to Benjamin's complex play of concepts and metaphors, its excesses and its silences, which he has already put on display in an exemplary way in "On Language." There the delimitation of human language as a naming language (*benennende Sprache*)— that is, Benjamin's emphatic resistance to identifying it with language tout court—leads to the recognition of the supreme point of tension of particular languages, in view of the divine word and in the name of the purity of language. Precisely this peculiar movement is what has led me to arrange as I have the texts I analyse: translation itself is what Benjamin thinks to be the determining factor of the essence of language, of all language. And if poetry is, presumably, the purest sphere of the human language of names, the problem of its translation should be, in all certainty, an unavoidable key to the deepest inquiry into this essence.[16]

However, this does not mean that the phenomenon of translation disappears into a universal and abstract totality, no matter how convincing its speculative force might be. On the contrary, Benjamin wants to hang on to its strict specificity. That is, he seeks to conceive of this specificity as an exceptional example of a situation where the encryption of the secret of language and languages can be found. From this point of view, the preface pursues two objectives that are indissociably linked. First, he means to establish a concept of translation that determines translation on the basis of what we might call its a priori basis, translatability. The latter is understood through the kinship of languages in their relation to pure language. Second, he proposes a way of understanding the practice of translation on the basis of this concept, in view of the two paradigmatic dilemmas of that practice: fidelity and freedom. Although the two objectives are connected, there is an essential discord between them, and this discord itself, as a proxy for impossibility, configures the matrix of Benjamin's insight into, and style in, the practice of translation. The title of the essay already implies this, and we must pay attention to it before all else. In truth, he expresses this discord paradoxically, as an indissociable alliance of elements that struggle to separate themselves. "The Task of the Translator," "Die Aufgabe des Übersetzters": the concept of *Aufgabe* is an imposition that is at the same time renunciation and failure, in other words finitude, obligation, contract, and promise that one is condemned to leave unfulfilled. And it is sealed by an irreducible duplicity.[17] This duplicity is all the more irreducible as it is the originary unfolding of something that, in itself, is one and the same but does not allow itself to be experienced other than as being double. But I will speak of this later. For the time being, suffice it to say that *reading* this text by Benjamin—and, in a certain way, any text by him—means committing oneself to thinking this irreducible duplicity.

"The Task of the Translator" begins by calling into question the concept of communication as transmission of *something* to *someone*. It is relatively easy to dismiss this notion in relation to the (poetic) original, which is essentially indifferent to its eventually informative import and inscrutable when it comes to the problem of its reception.[18] But this does not seem to be the case with the translation. Benjamin's intention is, nevertheless, to emphasize that translation cannot be conceived of as communication either. It is obvious that this concept is interpreted here with the help of the definition of "through" that the earlier essay offered. This implies that the translation, and not only the original, would have to be understood in the same way as the communication expression "in" explained in that essay: that is, in terms of mediality. However, it would be more appropriate to think that what Benjamin undertakes here—in conformity with the separation between translation and meaning, and to an extent that we will have to specify—is the displacement of the concept of translation itself toward the absolute center of linguistic relations. It is true that this displacement could be considered already produced at the end of the reflections in the second essay, particularly if we take into

account the meaning that the activity of translating takes
on in the recapitulation of the thesis at the end of this text.
But, precisely in this sense, it would be sound to argue
that the concept of communication, used strategically by
Benjamin to open and, so to speak, to measure the scope
of the theory of language, has been able to be definitively
eliminated and replaced by the concept of translation. It
is now a matter of freeing translation completely from
any submission to content, of letting it unfold purely as a
characterization of the performative essence of language,
if we can call it that.

I was speaking of Benjamin's interest in determining the
a priori basis of translation. This foundation, as *form*—
and not as simple act—must rest on the *translatability* of
the original. "If translation is a form, translatability must
be an essential feature of certain works" (GS IV.1 10, GS
I 254). The problem that this sentence contains requires
that it be resolved in an apodictic manner, Benjamin says.
On the one hand, while the character of apodicticity can
be conveniently collected from the reference to an a priori
of translation that is already expressed in the epistemological idea of an essential translat*ability*, this character is
not exhausted in the sphere of this reference. This is what
the appeal to the law indicates, and we should consider
the law inseparable from the definition of translation as
form: "To comprehend it as such, one must go back to the
original, for the laws governing the translation lie within
the original, contained in the issue of its translatability"
(GS IV.1 9, SW I 254, modified). And it is crucial to
understand that this law does not have to be conceived of
merely as the principle that circumscribes the limits of the
possibility of translation, represented as a possibility and
faculty susceptible, in a human way, of being documented.
On the contrary, the deepest meaning of the law—and, in
truth, it is only by virtue of this that a law is a law in the
strict sense—rests in the fact that it would make translation thinkable in its very impossibility, as a condition

of all human translation. Thus, just as it is appropriate to think of something essentially unforgettable even though all human beings might have forgotten it, one could appeal to a domain in which this unforgettable essence might find its match, "God's remembrance." Thus, too, "the translatability of linguistic creations ought to be considered even if human beings should prove unable to translate them. Given a strict concept of translation, would they not really be translatable to some degree?" (GS IV.1 10, SW I 254, modified). "A strict concept" is here a concept subjected to the constriction of the law, to its imperative efficacy: the law itself does not have an epistemological application but one of a different kind, which for the moment we might call ethical, even at the risk of some ambiguity.

In a sense that I assume is obvious, the question that governs the considerations put forward in this preface is analogous with or equivalent to the one that could be glimpsed from "On Language." If the latter was about figuring out in what sense communication is necessary to being, that is, to what extent there is a communicability *of* being (objective genitive), here we want to know to what extent translation is necessary to the original, that is, to what extent there is a translatability *of* the original. This necessity points, of course (as I just observed), to demand, to the command imposed by a law as law; we would have to know how the law that dictates translation (if there is one) operates already in the original. And we can already glimpse the sense in which the solution to this problem should be apodictic. At bottom, the law that dictates translation into the original and from it could not be other than inseparable from the relation that the original has, in its particular language, with the law—the relationship with the law that keeps that original in its particular language. And perhaps that law is nothing but this relation, this compromise.

One could believe that the equivalence I have just sketched out is merely formal. In a certain sense it is.

However, it ceases to have this aspect insofar as it attends to the essential move according to which Benjamin thinks the necessity to which I have referred. If I may be permitted to describe it this way, it is an undaunted necessity.

> Translatability is an essential quality of certain works, which is not to say that it is essential for the works themselves that they be translated; it means, rather, that a specific significance inherent in the original manifests itself in its translatability. It is evident that no translation, however good it may be, can have any significance as regards the original. Nonetheless, it does stand in the closest relationship to the original by virtue of the original's translatability; in fact, this connection is all the closer since it is no longer of importance to the original. We may call this connection a natural one, or, more specifically, a vital one. Just as the manifestations of life are intimately connected with the phenomenon of life without being of importance to it, a translation issues from the original—not so much from its life as from its afterlife. For a translation comes later than the original, and since the important works of world literature never find their chosen translators at the time of their origin, their translation marks their stage of continued life. (GS IV.1 10–11, SW I 254)

This necessity would be undaunted because nothing adds to the "life" itself of the work, which rests for the moment within itself. Instead, the work unfolds exclusively in the "afterlife." Life, however, is the seed of the work and, to this extent, the originality of the original. Just as the communicability of being means *nothing* for being (just as being can never be signified as mere being, but rather only inasmuch as it is a communicable being), translation does not make the work "live" any more within itself. But communicability belongs to being: being is being called, as we saw. In the same way, translation belongs to the original; the latter's translatability is nothing but its necessity to exteriorize its signification as life, or, better yet, its life as signification. The law of translatability is

precisely this exteriorization—or, even more precisely, it is
the law that dictates such an exteriorization already in the
original. For this reason, the undaunting necessity I speak
of is not a sterile necessity, but rather one over which reigns
the most fertile richness of germination; of translation it
will be said that its mission is "ripening the seed of pure
language" (GS IV.1 17, SW I 259). Paradoxically, then,
but at the same time rigorously, the afterlife, which means
nothing for the life of the original, is nonetheless the only
space in which the signification of that life can unfold. To
state this from the point of view of the work, the afterlife
is the space in which the relationship of the work with the
law must ripen. Afterlife and continued life are, for this
reason, an *increase* in life that adds signification to life;
they are the space and time of *tending* being, of serving
as an *auxiliary*, as long as we understand this word and
its roots in *augere*, "to increase." Benjamin will insist on
the theme of growth (*Wachstum*) and, furthermore, on the
"hallowed growth of languages" (GS IV.1 14, SW I 257).
The law of translatability is, from this point of view, the
law of the auxiliary construed as the law of signification
(*Bedeutung*).

But this increase implies death.

Perhaps comprehension of this conceptual knot can
be helped by a thesis on the difference between allegory
and symbol that the youthful Benjamin delved into, in
a discussion of Romantic theory that he carried out in
connection with his exposition on German baroque tragedy
[*Trauerspiel*]. Friedrich Creuzer and Johann Joseph Görres
are called on to bear witness, and it is precisely the introduction of temporality in the domain of semiotics, in the
name of "the great Romantic intuition of these thinkers,"
that provides the key to this difference. To the extent that
the symbol can be measured by the "mystic instant" in
which it shelters meaning in its hidden intimacy, allowing
redemption to flash meteorically on the face of nature,
allegory presents the face of history hollowed out by the

constant imminence [*perentoriedad*] of death, in such a way that history can have a meaning only on condition that everything eventually expires. It is "only meaningful in the stations of its decline," Benjamin asserts, and he adds: "So much meaning, so much forfeiture to death, for at the deepest level death incises the jagged line of demarcation between *phusis* and meaning" (GS I.1 343, O 174).

This lesson, I suppose, allows us to understand the paradox of afterlife, insofar as it determines this "after-" on the basis of the ineludible condition of mortality. What is at stake here is a radical conception of the finitude of being—a conception that relies on being's fundamental and irreducible multiplicity and diversity. Under the primacy of this finitude, signification is, at once, rescue of the fractured being and acceptance of its own fragility: all signification carries with it an essential trait of resignation—or mourning, if you will. This is what I had in mind when I mentioned a notion of the auxiliary. But, in addition, the passage emphasizes the historicity of the "after." Death is the condition that makes signification possible, as long as we understand that this condition is itself temporized: signification itself emerges in the ripeness of death. This moment of ripeness, this time, is the installation of history as the unfolding—a virtual one, at least—of significance in the heart of natural becoming, marked by its inevitable expiration.

For this reason, the law of signification is also a law of history. After all—to return to Benjamin's prologue to his translation of Baudelaire—it does not seem that we can understand completely the process of signification at the core of the relationship that characterizes translation (and generally at the core of the linguistic relationship), unless we dwell on the fact that this process is the primitive opening of the historical. Benjamin warns us emphatically that the process of thinking about life and about the continued life of artistic works need not be considered a simple metaphorical chat—in the way, we might say, the "bourgeois conception" understands metaphors; that, in truth, life is determinable only in an impoverished way, on the basis of soul and sensation; and that the appropriate jurisdiction for this concept is found primarily in the historical, which in turn manifests itself much more clearly in the lasting existence of works than in the fluctuating existence of creatures. In fact Benjamin makes use of the notion of life as a sort of rotating platform that spins, of course, in a vertiginous way. Introduced at the beginning by analogy—translation is to the original as exteriorization is to the living—this notion is the axis that allows the transition from nature to history, from history to language. The vertiginous quality of this movement causes it to lose all control, above all because every new turn crystallizes the former one without losing sight of it; and through this movement the initial analogy is sent back to its origins (and in this way it is suppressed, like an extrinsic equivalence). To this extent, life essentially remains in its reference to language, where all the paths cross that have been opened for work to be carried out on the problem of translatability. Language is the place of being; it is the entire topos of being, primarily because it is in language that the tangential relationship of being and signification opens up, as an intensive unfolding of language in the multiplicity and diversity of languages. There is therefore an essential and intimate (*innerstes*) link between these two elements, "a peculiar convergence. This special kind of kinship holds because languages are not strangers to one another, but are, a priori and apart from all historical relationships, interrelated in what they want to express (*in dem verwandt sind, was sie sagen wollen*)" (GS IV.1 12, SW I 255). This is the convergence that makes translation present, in a seminal way, as chiasma and crystal of the relationships that traverse it, as a place of transition, which nonetheless leaves its mark: "all translation is only a somewhat provisional way (*eine irgendwie vorläufige Art*) of coming to terms with the foreignness of languages. An instant and final rather than a temporary and provisional solution to this foreignness remains out of the reach of human beings; at any rate, it eludes any direct attempt" (GS IV.1 14, SW I 257, modified). This provisional solution (and salvation, which is also rescue from the provisional qua provisional) is indelible, because only in it—thanks to its more genuine movement, which is not derivative but points backward—is the kinship of languages subscribed, the air that blows across them all in spite of their mutual strangeness, looming over them like a consummation that is only felt as a premonition (*Ahnung*).

I spoke about history, and it is important to emphasize that this theme—which in "On Language" remained in a state of (suggestive) latency—is explicitly addressed in "The Task." It is true that the passage I quoted above and Benjamin's appeal to the "supra-historical" might seem to excuse me from considering it. But I believe that this hesitation is constitutive of the concept of history that Benjamin has begun to elaborate and that in this case is organized by a messianic motif. History itself would be made out of a merely provisional stuff, which is simultaneously a differing and a deferring [*un diferimiento*]. Translation shows this to be true. If it takes its departure from the original's sur-vival [*sobre-vida*], it has its origin not only in the distance that separates it from the original (without that the truth of the original is inane), but above all in how differing and deferring belong in the relationship between the original—in its own language—and the law. History would be the differing and deferring of the law, the incommensurable sphere that the fulfillment of the law would suppress to the extent that law—its irresistible advent—would be the end of history. And if translation comes after the original in the strict sense that it endorses its historicity, it is in translation that the relationship with the law comes more clearly into its own.

But what do we understand here by the term "law" [*"ley"*]? In truth, we have already seen it: it is the intimate kinship of languages, the sameness of their intended meanings, their wanting to say [*querer decir*], the fact that they, beyond the elements that make them up and that exclude each other mutually, "supplement (*ergänzen*) one another in their intentions" (GS IV.1 13, SW I 257). Later on, the idea of complementation and the fragment will be condensed in the image of a vessel whose shards, although variable among themselves (just as a translation need not be, nor can be, a copy of the original), fit in minutely among themselves, although they do so only tangentially, of course. If there is an idea of totality, it cannot be derived from any intra-worldly instance. Rather totality and the world itself are what throbs, almost imperceptibly, in the dissemination of linguistic modes. Translation provides an auxiliary, announcing totality and the world in a provisional way. The fragmentary and the fugitive appear here as indices of being, as historical being. The mark of being is never present to itself; is always different from, and deferred from, itself. It is finitude: it consists in nothing but being positioned on the edge of its own disappearance, in danger. Surely for this reason translation appeared to Benjamin as one of the basic models of historical relations, like criticism, collecting, and quotation. It is a rescue of being in the instant of its abolition, a rescue that must preserve being intact.

The law of translatability is the secret movement of the kinship and completion or complementation of languages. Benjamin writes: "this *Gesetz*, one of the fundamental laws of the philosophy of language" (GS IV.1 14, SW 257, modified). It defines the translation's position vis-à-vis the original, vis-à-vis the work, whose signification is precisely not the content of its possible communication, but rather its inscription in the historical and messianic process of the kinship of languages. This is what translators presuppose and cultivate, what is their task. This inscription is what translators take as their point of departure—an unavoidable signpost. No translation, no

effort or plan to translate would be possible if it did not
presuppose this law of affinity—if it did not presuppose,
that is, as what this law was tasked to symbolize. But
this undermines the traditional desire, which demands
that translators reproduce meaning. As the mode in
which each particular language says "the same," meaning
compels the particular language to remain within the
tenacious sphere of its exclusivity. Benjamin has recourse
here to phenomenology's reiteration of the scholastic
term *intentio* and, particularly, to the distinction it makes
between what is mentioned and the mode of mentioning.
While the former is the same for any particular language,
the latter—the mode or the meaning (*Sinn*)—constitutes
the diversity of languages. The task of the translator is
to intervene in this diversity, even though she or he does
so only in order to arrange for its absolution, its reconciliation (*Versöhnung*). The fact that what is mentioned
should be the same evokes what was at the center of the
essay on language: the grounding of a naturalist theory of
the name. But we should be clear about the scope of this
theory. Let us consider Plato's *Cratylus*, with which this
prologue has some connections. The identity of what is
mentioned is not that of something that would count as
an adequate object of knowledge. Benjamin avoids both
Cratylus's conviction that naming encloses [*encierra*] some
knowledge of the thing named and Socrates's thesis that it
presupposes knowledge and that the name is "by nature"
(*phusei*) the thing itself, graspable without and before
any linguistic relation.[19] On the contrary, knowledge is
that which can never be presupposed in the finite horizon
of human language. It is what naming provides as the
primordial act of translation. "On Language" remarked
on this via the theory of the proper name.[20] Thus the
thing mentioned is itself the fleeting, that which can never
be captured in a particular language but can be foretold
in the play of linguistic resonance, which points toward
the place of its advent. It is not modeled on cognition

but on revelation (*Offenbarung*), which, by the way, was
also in the background of the 1916 essay on language.
Epistemology takes the form of apocalyptic vision. And
here is the decisive point, which dissolves the conflict
between naturalism and conventionalism in the concept
of translation.[21] In general, that which is self-identical and
properly itself is not a thing but linguistic speech [*lengua*]
itself, pure language [*lengua pura*], the word of God,
the letter of the law, but at the same time the complementary diversity of languages, of the shards, as a pure
space of resonance.[22] The problem of the homologation
of language and being, or the problem of their difference,
gets settled in this way, by establishing that they are indistinguishable in the reciprocal tension that links them to
the law. The sameness that is mentioned *is* not, in any of
the senses in which the word is said; nor is it *said*, in any
of the modes of saying. And this is the same as saying that
the sameness "is" the other in a radical way: it "is" the
referral of being to the law. We can only translate it; it is
precisely something that is not in our power.

The title of Benjamin's preface already announced this;
it is a title that prefaces the preface, so much so that it
indicates ahead of time everything that is to be said.

On the one hand, *Aufgabe* is task: a task as charge, as
a gift (*Gabe*) imposed, which assigns a destiny. Something
should be given on the basis of which translation begins,
from which its process is initiated. Something should
be given as the origin of translation; something like the
original should be given. *It should* be given, so that it
might be possible to give it once again (*wiedergeben*), to
render it: to translate. And, if it is impossible in general
that an original might give itself to the one who wants
to give it once again (assuming that his or her proper
role is to withdraw or herself from it), the effect of the
origin remains guaranteed without appeal, to the extent
that what is given is constituted through a demand. The
gift imposed, then, is also imperative; it is a command:

what is given is handed down and handed over [*legado y delegado*]. The translator finds her- or himself, then, subject to the command—that is, to the dictates—of that which is given to her or him to translate, what is given for translation, committed to an act of caring: the care for what has been handed down and handed over [*lo [de] legado*].

But *Aufgabe* is also renunciation, abandonment. The demand of what has been given—the dictates of the gift, the dictate that the gift consists of—constitutes and institutes translation itself, and defines the mission (delivery, assignment, message) of the translator. This demand is determined in the translator, but also before the translator, by a renunciation that is equally constitutive. This means, rigorously, that translation is impossible.

What is the nature of this impossibility? Perhaps it is not too fanciful to assume that it is captured by the idea of *traduttore, traditore* ["the translator is a traitor"]. Benjamin does not mention it but it could plausibly be read between the lines of his text, owing to the unbearable tension between fidelity and freedom thought of as the tangential relationship in the infinitesimal point of meaning. This directs us to an understanding of what betrayal means here.[23] At first glance, it is obvious: every translator is condemned to betray what she or he translates, because it is impossible to deliver the same thing, qua the same, to the other. But this only manages to stipulate the limit, the restrictive, intolerable finitude of translation. It does not specify the crime or explain the fault. For this we need an option, a will, a decision; translation's betrayal would grow out of the will to translate. This will would find itself squeezed in the grip of the lethal alternative between spirit and letter, content and form, meaning and syntax, fidelity and freedom. It would be forced to choose, at every step, in an infinitesimal way. The will feels the urge to leap over the sometimes imperceptible abyss that separates these conceptual partners, an abyss that, in any case, is impossible to identify or situate. This sentence, this destiny inevitably leads the translator back to betrayal, to guilt, and to chance; to the impossibility of the task. If we look at it in a different way, in order to *be able* to translate one would have not to have *wanted* to translate. A strict paradox, which assigns the translator something impossible yet feasible: the forging of a decision out of hesitation.[24] From Benjamin's perspective, this is perhaps what Hölderlin accomplishes in his translations of Sophocles: "in them meaning plunges from abyss to abyss, until it threatens to become lost in the bottomless depths of language" (GS IV.1 21, SW I 262).[25] Benjamin recalls that these are Hölderlin's final work before he recedes into the twilight. That is, Hölderlin wavers on the threshold of insanity. The impossibility to which that paradox commits the translator is that of no longer being a subject, no longer clinging to the particularity of a being born in the sphere of a mother tongue, with a historical predicament, a national and cultural community, a race, a class, an interest, a desire, a fortuitous journey through life, while the translator is nevertheless under the spell of all this particularity and obliged to speak to it.

What if betrayal were understood not as a defect that comes from the particularity of one worldview but rather as something that a priori constitutes languages, nationalities, cultures, interests, and subjects? What might an a priori betrayal be? Without deciding whether there can be an answer to this question, I would venture to argue that Benjamin's suggestion points in this direction. In effect, if what I have just highlighted in the foregoing is valid, if betrayal truly germinates in the will to translate and if the possibility of translation lies in renouncing this will, then, in the first place, renunciation belongs to the essence of translation. However, this does not mean that the betrayal could be evaded through some sort of abstention—which, as a result, could offer only the factical irreality of translation. In the same way, renunciation does not require that one presuppose the previous effectiveness of the will to translate. The problem is more complex and its complexity is ineradicable, that of a structural duplicity that unfolds in a structural way, without end. To articulate it in an efficient way, which verges on the permissible limits of simplification, let me say the following: the command by which translation is constitutively bound, the gift of that which is yet to be translated [*lo por-traducir*], prescribes the will to translate as renunciation of itself. Both will and renunciation are indistinguishable and ineradicable.[26] One can translate only when one does not want to translate: this phrase expresses the renunciation in which translation consists; and said renunciation is prescribed in the gift and by the gift itself. One can translate to the extent that one accepts the gift, and one accepts the gift to the extent that one renounces it, that is, in proportion with one's experience of the gift from the reserve whence it gives itself. Only by renouncing the gift does one accept it as a gift. Only by accepting it like this is it possible to give it back. Only in this way is the *Wiedergabe* of translation possible. Translation derives its possibility from the wellspring of the translatable, which is the untranslatability at the core of the translatable, and that is the incommunicable or, to put it another way, the demand that something should remain intact. Thus renunciation *is* the essence of translation, since the gift itself unfolds in itself, in reserve and in renunciation. All along the edge and through the narrow passage of this duplicity are arrayed the infinitesimal tangential points that, according to Benjamin, characterize translation qua translation.

Might it be the case, then, that translation *is* not? Maybe it *is* not, but rather it is *owed*.

Finally, Benjamin's agonizing over translation has to serve as a preamble to the work he did with some of Baudelaire's poems. This work remains subjected, then, to the unheard of criterion that defines his reflections. Conversely, it also offers an example of his compliance or failure in the attempt to comply. Of course, Benjamin does not allude to his translations in his prologue. He limits himself to placing his reflections before the poems, as if confident that the elucidation of what is said and what is done might appear from the contiguity of the two spaces. Certainly his versions of the *Tableaux parisiens* have the uncanny strictness of balancing on an edge where fidelity is not sacrificed in favor of liberty; nor is the latter injured by adherence to the former. The two complement each other in order to allow the peculiar, jagged music of Baudelaire's voice, in which the light touch and the tangential character of the infinitesimal point of meaning is bound to make itself sensible and audible.

A possible objection appears to repeat a strategy of the text, which seems to dismiss its own speculations as vain digressions, so that, when all is said and done, they wind up within the sphere of the habitual vision of translation. According to such an objection, one could argue that the system of displacements and paradoxes that the prologue skillfully ties together has served only to create predispositions for a reading of translations that, even if they are brilliant, are hardly unique in their genre. But I think his own translations are not what Benjamin would recommend as the paradigm for his doctrine. The paradigms (for they are more than one) should be sought in the essay itself. Without a doubt, the end mentions "the interlinear version of the Scriptures (as) the prototype or ideal of all translation" (GS IV.1 21, SW I 263). The latter is perhaps the fulfillment of the tangential nature of trans-lation. The proposal for this archetype sounds paradoxical, certainly, and this seems to lie at the center of Benjamin's concern about translation. We would have to assume, too, that Hölderlin's versions of Greek poetry, and especially his abysmal translations of Sophocles, belong to such an archetype. They are just as paradoxical: illegible at the time of their composition and problematic for posterity, they have generated, above all, silence. And, finally, we would have to add to these that other model that Benjamin mutely inscribes at the center of his prologue, an inaudible step from one language to another, when he quotes a celebrated passage from Mallarmé's *Crise de vers* without translating it: "languages are imperfect in that although there are many, the supreme one is lacking: thinking is to write without accessories, or whispering, but since the immortal word is still tacit, the diversity of tongues on the earth keeps everyone from uttering the word which would be otherwise in one unique rendering, truth itself in its substance" (GS IV.1 17, SW I 259).[27] Just as genuine translation *avant la lettre* refers both the word it renders and its own word to a "greater language" of which the two are fragments, this quotation lovingly preserves the shred it takes over, opening it to the secret posteriority of its signification. Quotation is, then, a model of translation.[28] The quotation mediates, says Benjamin, between poetry and doctrine, which it brings together, assigning to philosophy its task and its strict law. Philosophy would be the promise and commitment of yearning for "that language [the language of truth that is the true language] which manifests itself in translation" (GS IV.1 17, SW I 259, modified).

Conclusion

In the introductory part of this essay I attempted to suggest that the determining scenario for contemporary philosophy's reflections and inquiries could be described as a quest for the "linguistic totalization" of the questions that concern it. In fact these reflections are nothing new; precedents can be found anywhere in the past hundred or so years, and their explicit verification has been underway for a long time, throughout the second half of the twentieth century. I also hinted—although not as clearly, and I would now like to provide more details—that one could

distinguish two phases of this totalization. The first could
be characterized by a postulate of coextensivity—isomorphism or sameness—between being and language. With
this postulate the western discourse of ontology reaches
its fulfillment—a discourse that has been supported from
the start by the articulation (in final analysis, residual)
of *to on* ["being"] and *logos*. I say this because, in any
case, that which has been called *to on* prevails, for this
discourse, as the inexhaustible horizon of all references
and all capacities of language, be it conceived of as origin
(*archē*) or as end (*telos*). The coextensivity that has been
postulated tends either to suppress the reserve in which
"being" holds itself for such a discourse or to make it
evident only as an insignificant residue. To some extent,
the overcoming of ontology is sketched out consistently
as the fundamental form of discourse in philosophy. This
overcoming is undertaken in the second phase of the
totalization I am speaking of, by way of an analysis of
language as praxis that resolves all those instances that
had been fixed by ontology as markers of the knowledge
of and reference to being, in a general process of linguistic
performance. Thus, "being" itself is outdone in favor of
an understanding of the *eventual* as that which reigns and
unfolds in the immanent interconnection of performances.
Consequently, in order to distinguish it specifically from
the first phase, this second phase, to which I have attributed
a radical character, could be construed as a "performative
totalization." Speaking of "totalization" seems to me
permissible, in spite of the degree of openness that we
might ascribe to the central postulate of this second phase
or to its multiple applications and variations. After all, in
some way, what is essentially at stake is the affirmation
of a comprehensive sufficiency of linguistic praxes for the
sake of an approach to, or clearing up of, fundamental
philosophical questions.

    If what I have said is correct and if there is a place for
the question I formulated at the beginning as a sort of

framework or guideline for my reading of two of Benjamin's early essays, if there is any validity to asking these texts the question about the relationship between language and being that the texts themselves might be said to pose, it must be possible to sketch out an adequate answer.

As far as that goes, perhaps the most decisive peculiarity of the young Benjamin's meditation on language, considered in the context of "performative totalization," consists precisely in the resistance to totalization itself.

It is true that Benjamin's deliberations could be convincingly supported from a performative perspective. To perceive this clearly, it is enough to ask in what way we should construe what the texts refer to by the name "pure language." In spite of what one might suppose on coming across the issue for the first time, as more than one reader has proposed, this name does *not* refer back nostalgically to some kind of primordial identity that one might attempt to restore, reducing the Babelesque linguistic and historical dispersion to the point of abolishing it. I have insistently tried to show the delicate, painstaking care that Benjamin devotes to understanding language on the basis of the particularity of individual languages. If this particularity indicates imperfection, the latter is not regarded as a deficiency but as a condition without which purity is inconceivable. To put it another way, "pure language" would be nothing but the *free* deployment of the partial and imperfect languages of human beings. Free because it is no longer rigid or discordant, but harmonious and complementary. This deployment is what translation announces, and in such a way that the translatability of texts is like the glimpse of an unlimited *translativity* [*traductividad*], which, by the way, no longer recognizes any pre-text.[29] And, of course, such a translativity might seem to offer a worthy variant of the "performative totalization" I have discussed.

Nevertheless, I want to emphasize one other thing. At the point where this variant appears, there also emerges

a resistance to the totalization I mentioned. Because in
Benjamin there is a conception of reserve: we have to
run across it through the themes of the uncommunicable,
the non-symbolizable, and the intangible, for example.
Except that, in the same vein as what I have just pointed
out, this reserve does not correspond—as happens with
the metaphysical concept of reserve—to an original or
teleological fullness. It has to do instead with interruption,
lapse, and the suspension characteristic of radical incom-
municability and inexpressivity, radical non-presence.
Such a lapse takes away from performances precisely that
which totality depends on, that is, its efficacy—the efficacy
of performances. And for this reason it emphasizes the
trait of the eventual, of which performances are bearers.
We are therefore dealing with a reserve without effect,
which corresponds to Benjamin's specific version of *sōzein
ta phainomena* ["saving the appearances/phenomena"],
that is, to his impulse to oppose any idea or principle of
continuity (whether it relates to causation or to semiosis)
insofar as it involves the obliteration of particularity and
alterity in anything that might happen, the flattening out
of what has been and what is possible against the picture
window of the present moment. All communication and
all expression verge on this moment of interruption,
in such a way that unlimited translativity—the realm
of pure language—is not the immanent and, to put it
one way, the narcissistic play of a merely unleashed
eloquence. On the contrary, translatability is the interminable mourning of the finitude of being, where mourning
itself (the feasible diversity of the *logoi* ["discourses"] of
individual languages) is, precisely, what makes finitude
apparent as that which first institutes being. What is at
stake here, I believe, is a notion of truth abstracted from
any notion of efficacy, undaunted, foreign to all measures
of performance, unproductive; a truth that is stranger to
any archeology or teleology of production. But this would
require another analysis.

In any case, this truth carries the mark of death. It is on the basis of this mark that Benjamin interrupts rather than overcomes the discourse of ontology. And he interrupts it indefinitely. I say it in this way because I think that it would not be wrong to argue that, instead of accomplishing an overcoming of ontology as the fundamental inherited format of all discourse, Benjamin undertakes to induce a *separation* within ontology, an internal separation: onto/logy. The illegible bar that separates is that mark, which suggests that the possibility (forever deferred) of saying "being" arises from the open hiatus between the two, experienced at the same time as death and as the announcement of the law, that is, as the irruption of otherness and the other.

Lima, Santiago, August 1990

2

Four Suggestions about Experience, History, and Facticity in the Thought of Walter Benjamin[*]

The First Suggestion

The following "suggestions" concern primarily the celebrated "Theses on the Philosophy of History," as the work has customarily been called.[1] These suggestions (including this one) do not aim to induce a particular reading of the "theses"; nor do they provide commentary, in which case they would turn out to be too brief anyway. They were written with the conviction that it is not

[*] This essay served as introduction to an edition and translation of texts about Walter Benjamin's philosophy of history, published for the first time in 1996. That volume included, together with "On the Concept of History" (sometimes known as "Theses on the Philosophy of History") and its variants, Convolute N of the *Arcades Project*, and, as an appendix, the "Theological–Political Fragment." In the second edition, "Eduard Fuchs, Collector and Historian" was added as Appendix II. The original texts were taken from *Gesammelte Schriften* (I.2 691–704), as were the variants (GS I.3 1255–1257), and from the *Werke und Nachlaß* edition of "Über den Begriff der Geschichte," especially the manuscript of Benjamin's work (WN XIX 30–43). In English, "Eduard Fuchs" appears in SW III 260–302 and the "Theological–Political Fragment" in SW III 305–306; Convolute N is in A 457–488. While "Theses on the Philosophy of History" bears this title in the classic anthology *Illuminations* (edited by Hannah Arendt, translated by Harry Zohn, Schocken Books, 1968), in SW 388–400 it is published as "On the Concept of History."

possible, nor desirable, to enclose those texts in a system of legibility that has already been resolved. A quick glance at the different extant versions suffices to see that the number and their order vary. The instability of the whole can be confirmed by the various outlines and notes, although their center of gravity, however discreet, makes itself apparent in all the relevant materials. The multiple versions of the theses, which are as repetitious as they are digressive, reveal that their text is still, so to speak, pending and underway, in a process of being formed. Together with notes, reflections, and fragments that relate to them and in a certain way complement them, they are like the wake of a complex movement that, in the notoriously inconclusive trail they leave behind, wants and, indeed, manages to express this true center. This is an inalienable characteristic of Benjamin's thought, and it can be observed in his entire oeuvre. Think, for example, of the epistemological notes of Convolute N in the *Arcades Project*, which often touch on the themes of the theses.[2] These reflections serve as an accompaniment to the inquiry into the constitutive threshold of "modernity" that Benjamin undertakes in this literally uncontainable project; they provide indications of its orientation and a measure of its lucidity. In fact Benjamin did not come to specify the mode of this accompaniment; this is so for reasons that concern his completely singular procedure within philosophy, and I will return to this point in a moment. At the same time, if we consider the so-called "Theological–Political Fragment" (GS II.1 203–204, SW III 305–306), which goes back to an earlier period,[3] it is evident that the movement we mentioned traces a much broader arc than one might have thought at first sight: in truth, more than an arc, it is a braid whose strands converge from opposite extremes (let us say, to simplify, from the metaphysics of youth and the materialism of maturity) toward an unheard of crossing: the imminent arrival of the Messiah as the essential dynamic of history.

When I speak about this movement, I do not mean
exclusively Benjamin's stylistic and rhetorical peculiar-
ities, or the thematic texture of his discussions. I allude
rather to what we might call his method, to the paradox
of method that defines this author's absolutely original
philosophical inscription. An essential characteristic of
Benjamin's thought is his formulation of tasks whose
unrealizable character can be established in advance.
This procedure immediately defines his peculiar way of
understanding method in philosophy. The latter has been
traditionally conceived of as knowledge about principles
and epistemological problems, and for this reason it
constitutes the formal ground of the unity of the possible
contents of knowledge in a given realm. Meanwhile, in
Benjamin it acquires the meaning of a revindication of the
rights of knowable matter. The profound conviction called
for by this attitude toward method concerns essentially
the idea of truth that method implies. On the traditional
conception, method consists in the projection and securing
of the truth of the cognitions it makes accessible. This
idea, from Benjamin's point of view, is unilateral as much
as it is (literally) arbitrary: it leaves truth at the mercy
of method and its projective capacities. Thus it does
not seize the truth, but rather the representation that it
makes of the truth and that it proposes in place of what is
knowable. The dominant idea of method, which belongs
to an equally dominant philosophy, limits itself to precon-
ceiving the truth to a degree that suits the representation
of truth, that is, is in accord with the truth's intention,
with the will to truth. This idea forgets, precisely, what has
awoken this intention, again and again: a chance event, a
danger, a hunch, the obstinate coarseness of the real. In
this forgetting, injustice prevails, flagrantly. But proper
truth gets eclipsed by the patent character of injustice.
Perhaps it could be said that an alarming instance of this
obliteration is the one that reverberates inexorably in the
deep conviction that motivates Benjamin's thought and

is already expressed in his debate against the intentional determination of knowledge: this is an early debate that remains throughout his work. Truth requires "the death of intention."[4] Indeed, this peculiar form of annihilation does not suppress knowledge, although it transforms its nature. It does affect the will to dominate what is knowable, which inevitably carries out a preterition of the knowable in favor of installing knowledge in the present. Annihilation reveals itself, then, as a temporalization of knowledge and its truth, without reservations. Benjamin's concept of method is paradoxical in that it requires resigning the will to knowledge—without which not only method but knowledge itself would seem unthinkable—in favor of the irreplaceable singularity of what is known. Thus method wants to rectify the unilateral arbitrariness of the truth, establishing the indissociable link between truth and justice, even though it would be infinitely fragile in that it is made of time. The fundamental rule of this linkage—and hence also of the method that establishes it—might be articulated in these terms: if our knowledge does not do justice to what is known, it cannot claim truth for itself. It is precisely this requirement that defines knowledge as a rescue operation and designates redemption as a category—the highest one—of knowledge. True knowledge is redemptive knowledge.

Experience

Gershom Scholem explains that Benjamin composed the essay "On the Program of the Coming Philosophy" (GS II.1 157–171, SW I 100–110) in November 1917. As the title indicates, it is a text that attempts to define the fundamental tasks that contemporary philosophical reflection should take up in order to project itself historically, on the basis of a critical appropriation of its essential origin. The key to this program lies in the goal of unifying the demand for the *purest* legitimation of knowledge with the demand for the *deepest* concept of experience. In other words, it lies in the connection of the most epistemologically rigorous *form* with the *content* that is most intensely rich in determinations. To the extent that the demand for purity has found its highest instances in Plato and Kant, and especially in the latter,[5] the crucial problem is concentrated in the question of experience. Thus "the primary challenge faced by contemporary philosophy ... is, according to the typology of Kantian thought, to undertake the epistemological foundation of a higher concept of experience" (GS II.1 160, SW I 102). The decisive limitation of Kantian philosophy lies in the precariousness of the experience that provides material for its concept of knowledge: the mathematical–mechanical experience of nature, which has its most finished model in Newtonian physics. Benjamin ponders over a corrective that would consist in referring knowledge to language (something that Johann Georg Hamann had already attempted during Kant's lifetime)— that is, in conceiving of a linguistic essence of knowledge. This implies in turn rescuing language, too, from its mere empiricalness, as Benjamin effectively attempts to do in his remarkable essays "On Language in General and on the Language of Man," published in 1916, and "The Task of the Translator," published in 1923. In these essays the precariousness of an experience modeled on mechanisms is reflected in language by the debasement of the word in its integration into the context of "communication": mechanism and mercantilism are two aspects of the same constellation.[6] Re-elaborated in this way, the concept of experience finds its most elevated sphere and outline in religion—so much so that, according to these essays, the latter yields the purest relationship with the essence of language. "Thus, the demand upon the philosophy of the future can ultimately be put in these words: to create on the basis of the Kantian system a concept of knowledge to which a concept of experience corresponds, of which the knowledge is the teaching (*Lehre*)" (GS II.1 168, SW I 108). With regard to the question of experience, these are the terms in which Benjamin first treats the peculiar relationship between philosophy and theology that will preoccupy him in "On the Concept of History."[7]

The foregoing statements inevitably raise questions. What is the specificity of religious experience that allows it to be conceived of as the paragon of experience when examined at its deepest conceptual level? Or, in a different mode, how does Benjamin construe the notion of experience, in order to determine the differences between depth and "superficiality" (that is, a signification that approaches zero) of experience? What characteristics does this meditation attribute to experience? How can language be constituted as the guiding thread for the determination of these characteristics?

A preliminary but indispensable orientation is offered here by a review of the fundamental traits that philosophical thought has attributed to experience. At first glance, and in accordance with what interests me here, we can distinguish three such traits:

1. The first trait was established systematically by Aristotle. Experience is inscribed as a moment in the organic becoming of knowing, that is, in the genetic process of its structural characteristics. This is to some extent a paradoxical trait, since the two components that define it do not seem to go together at all. Considered genetically, experience requires the *repeatability* that belongs to memory: from *many* memories *an* experience is born. Nevertheless, in its structuring of knowledge, "experience [*empeiria*] is knowledge [*gnōsis*] of singulars [*tōn kath' hekaston*]."[8] From a logical point of view, what is defined here is the cognitive quantity of what can be experienced. But we should not lose sight of the inherent temporality of this notion, which, on account of memory's repeatability, refers to the past as

an eminent dimension. This past, however, is significant
(i.e. has value for knowledge) only to the extent that,
articulated in the commensurability of its pertinent
moments, it can serve as a criterion for decisions about
what is presented in the present. Accordingly, we can
say that the apparent paradox is resolved in the essential
form that experience assumes as knowledge and that we
can call the form of familiarity.

2. Ideally, we could say that the second characteristic
derives from the analysis of the mode of being of
the singular. If its being consists essentially in its
presentation—in its occurrence, its advent—then it is
contingent in a constitutive way. Even when what is
known by experience is configured on the basis of a
regularity that can be evoked (or of an evocation that
selects precisely what is regular), this regularity cannot
serve as a certain basis for the prediction of its own
non-exceptional prolongation in the future. The presentation of the singular marks the efficacy of a rupture of
the present, which renders the singular unadministrable
through common knowledge. This is the moment of
the birth of empiricism, which wants to do justice to
the emphatic meaning of experience and locates this
meaning, by right, in the moment of rupture, in which
knowledge knows itself to be dependent on the presentation of its content, its matter. Experience is, in this
sense, *unforeseeable*. In logical terms, this is about the
cognitive quality of the object of experience, which
allows an empiricist as well as a transcendental version
of itself. From one point of view, which it is not relevant
to the present dispute, I would be inclined to say that
it is in this last form—that is, in Kant, and particularly
in the *Critique of Judgement*—that the idea reached its
greatest acumen and that, consequently, the temporal
character of experience shows its most incisive point:
the place where one might strive to recognize the factor
of repetition puts on display a *difference* that cannot

be suppressed. In accordance with this difference, the present of presentation shows itself to be more the irruption of a not yet known future than the confirmation of a present that extends out of the past. Even so, the Kantian circumscription of this difference, this rupture, does not insist on its most abrupt power of dislocation and estrangement; rather Kant insists on its capacity to increase or open up the space of the familiar, the house of meaning.

3. The third characteristic was elaborated upon by Hegel above all, and concerns the "bearer" of the experience, the subject. Here it is a matter of the recognition that Hegel dedicates, in spite of all vehement criticism, to the "great principle" of empiricism, that is, to the argument that "whatever is true must be in the actual world and present to sensation."[9] This objective principle, according to which philosophy knows only what effectively *is*, and not what merely *should* be, has a subjective side, in accordance with which "the human being must see *for himself* and feel that he is present in every fact of knowledge which he has to accept."[10] The vigor of empiricism has its roots, then, in fidelity to the essential structure of experience. We could call the characteristic in which this structure is expressed *testimoniality*. It defines the cognitive quality of the very process of experience and should be understood as the most elemental reality of pure *presence*: knowledge that certifies the being (existence, *Dasein*) of an entity presupposes the being-there (existence, *Da[bei]sein*) of the subject, that is, the auto-certification of the subject.[11]

Singularity, unforeseeability, and testimoniality: here is a possible catalogue of the determining traits of the inherited concept of experience. If this perception is correct and they have not been described in too clumsy a manner, in the tradition's exegesis, they are dominated by a strong idea of presence and by a profound sense of identity. The

first fruits of the concept of experience that Benjamin
suggests break with this idea and with this sense. Taken
in its most general aspect, the fracture, of course, can be
attributed to an itch that nags certain philosophies of the
early twentieth century. As we can see in Bergson, Husserl,
Emil Lask, and the early Heidegger, there is an intensi-
fication of the question of true access to the immediacy
of experience as the event of reality's happening—to its
genuine condition and its original givenness. But Benjamin
does not seem to adopt the obligatory solution, which is to
place one's bets on the immanent categorial nature of lived
experience. Instead, he insists on the dislocating power of
experience, and on the indelible character of death at its
core: the signature of temporality, which cannot be appropriated and which death inscribes into being. If experience
must provide the dense significations that doctrine must
structure in a systematic way, it is necessary to admit that
it is the difference related to death that institutes what
occurs in the sphere of ideality. Regarding this difference
and its temporalizing efficacy, a decisive and often cited
passage from *Origin of German Tragic Drama* says:

> History, in everything untimely, sorrowful, and miscarried
> that belongs to it from the beginning, is inscribed in a face—
> no, in a death's head. And though it is true that to such a thing
> all "symbolic" freedom of expression, all classical harmony
> of form, and everything human is lacking, nevertheless in
> this figure, the most fallen in nature, is expressed meaning-
> fully as enigma not only the nature of human existence in
> general but the biographical historicity of an individual. This
> is the core of the allegorical vision, of the Baroque profane
> exposition of history as the Passion of the world—meaningful
> only in the stations of its decline. So much meaning, so much
> forfeiture to death, for at the deepest level death incises the
> jagged line of demarcation between physis and meaning. But
> if nature has at all times been subject to the power of death,
> it is also at all times allegorical. Meaning and death are
> brought to fruition in historical unfolding (*sind so gezeitigt in*

historischer Erfahrung), just as they are closely intermeshed as seeds in the unredeemed state of sin of the creature. (GS I.1 343, O 174)

The fundamental destructiveness of death—and the fact that, after all, it is not a mere tearing down from the outside but a muffled throbbing of decline that resonates in everything there is—establishes the condition that makes signification possible, as long as one understands that this condition is, in itself, temporalized. Precisely at the moment of death, under the sign of the posthumous, meaning arises. And precisely this moment, this time, the difference in which this time consists is the installation of history as the (at least virtual) unfolding of significance in the heart of natural becoming—a significance marked by its congenitally decaying destiny. Thus thinking history in its truth requires us to assume that death is the midwife of this truth to the extent that it traces out the character of what might happen, of that which, on the basis of its weak being, is already what has happened—not that which "is" in its fullness, but that which "was"; not what merely was, but what *has been* [*lo sido*]. But, for this very reason, thinking the historical truth demands that we keep open the posthumous aperture to signification, and do so out of knowledge that such an opening expires. As Benjamin argues in *Origin of German Trauerspiel* and in the writings on language that I referred to earlier, the figure for this emergence of signification is the name.

One could certainly point to death, to the essentially withering condition of that which "is," as the instant (*Augenblick*) of experience—as the thing that, without ever being a theme of experience, is nonetheless its irrevocable condition, the condition of its temporality. It ruptures, ahead of time, its categorial articulation and converts what would have been the continuous field of the subject's unfolding into an intersection of inevitable risk. It places the essence of *Erfahrung* in the imminence of danger

(*Gefahr*).[12] A glimpse of this connection is probably what
led the young Benjamin to privilege religious experience as
a paradigm of depth. Such a paradigm would consist, not
in the confident accentuation of the identity of the knower
but in the acute dislocation of the subject by virtue of her
access to the other, in the conversion of this subject—
who is certain of herself and secure in the mastery of her
familiar surroundings—into an other, aware that he will
expire and precarious for this very reason, yet passionately
tenacious in his care for his own poverty, which is his only
possession, and a problematic and paradoxical one at that.
One consequence is a fundamental change in the indices
of experience that we have gathered from the traditional
analysis: singularity becomes, in a manner of speaking,
macroscopic; the unforeseeable exceeds all comfort that
might be offered by virtuous analogies; testimony declares
the absence of the witness in the fleeting moment of the
test. Experience not only confronts us with the unprecedented: it changes us. It not only hands over to us the
material for knowledge: it is the condition for knowledge
to occur. It will therefore have the quality of striking
in its own way, with a transformative fit of dizziness
(as it were), the concept that might think experience
intensively—in its dizzying mutability, as it were. This
intensive notion would have to be situated in Benjamin's
allusion to religious experience.[13] The principle of religious
experience refers to what lies at the very origin of the
possibility of religation [*la religación*],[14] and above all to
the essential dynamic of experience itself. This principle
could be located with the help of a term that Benjamin
uses occasionally in his mature work: *Einfall*—being
assaulted by radical alterity as that which has irrevocably
determined me while it was withdrawing from the capital
of my present knowing. Benjamin's conviction about this
dynamic refutes all possibility of bringing what has been
experienced to the stability of a categorial framework or
of a transcendental order. For the mature Benjamin, it

will become clear that the dynamic has the quality of a *shock*, and its effect is the kind of hallucinatory turn that belongs not to the mystical center of religion but to the purely borderline experience of waking up. Concerning this experience, concerning the disturbing temporality that links it to the eminently historical function of memory, it is worth quoting two fragments from the *Arcades Project*:

> The Copernican revolution in historical perception is as follows. Formerly it was thought that a fixed point had been found in "what has been," and one saw the present engaged in tentatively concentrating the forces of knowledge on this ground. Now this relation is to be overturned, and what has been is to become the dialectical reversal (*Umschlag*)—the flash (*Einfall*) of awakened consciousness. Politics attains primacy over history. The facts become something that just now first happened to us, first struck us; to establish them is the affair of memory. Indeed, awakening is the great exemplar of memory: the occasion on which it is given to us to remember what is closest, tritest, most obvious. What Proust intends with the experimental rearrangement of furniture in matinal half-slumber, what Bloch recognizes as the darkness of the lived moment, is nothing other than what here is to be secured on the level of the historical, and collectively. There is a not-yet-conscious knowledge (*Noch-nicht-bewußtes-Wissen*) of what has been; its advancement (*Förderung*) has the structure of awakening. (GS V.1 1491–492, A 388–389)

> There is a wholly unique experience of dialectic. The compelling—the drastic—experience, which refutes everything "gradual" (*"allgemach"*) about becoming and shows all seeming "development" to be dialectical reversal, eminently and thoroughly composed, is the awakening from dream. For the dialectical schematism at the core of this process, the Chinese have often found, in their fairy tales and novellas, a highly pregnant expression. The new, dialectical method of doing history presents itself as the art of experiencing the present as waking world, a world to which that dream we name the past refers in truth. To pass through and

carry out (*durchzumachen*) *what has been* in remembering
the dream!—Therefore: remembering and awakening are
most intimately related. Awakening is namely the dialectical,
Copernican turn of remembrance. (GS V.1 492, A 389)[15]

Benjamin will not cease to work on the idea of this experiential intensity, resisting the threat of a cloudy vision that
appears from its euphoric side and sharpening its critical
edge. In precisely this sense, he will convert the secular
and almost enlightened (so to speak) version of intensity
that the religious implied for him in his youth into the
model of awakening we find in his maturity. This change
was doubtless induced by a Proustian search; but surre-
alism plays a considerable part in it too. At stake here is
the crystallization of that intensity, and not merely being
frightened by it. This crystallization, its process, and the
multiplicity of its fractures and reflective surfaces mark the
linguistic nature of the experience. The crystal is made of
words, which converge in the lucidity of the image. And
the images—in which one finds concentrated the macroscopic effect of waking up, that is, the insistence of the
singular as an outgrowth of otherness—converge in their
turn, asymptotically, toward something Benjamin always
cautioned us about as the pure place of the other—a place
that cannot be appropriated, that keeps our experience
and our language in suspense: the Name.

History

In the first thesis Benjamin refers to the story of von
Kempelin's puppet: a simulated automaton with which von
Kempelin traveled from city to city, challenging all those
who wanted to prove their talent in a game of chess. This
happened in the second half of the eighteenth century. The
date is not insignificant. It is the dawning of technological
modernity, which begins to show its dominating power

in the model of the *machine* and to disclose its utopian dreams in the paradox of the self-moving apparatus, perpetuum mobile—is an analogue of life. Nevertheless, for von Kempelen and his wonder, technique does not consist in machinery but in *mimēsis*. As an automaton, the puppet is a fraud. Of course, it takes the design and construction of a system of mirrors to accomplish the deception and keep the chess-playing dwarf safe within its hidden chamber. And a mechanism that secretly controls the movements of a rigid doll is also required. Technique is not absent; but it is only in the service of illusion. As simulacrum of an automaton, von Kempelen's Turk is the anticipatory imitation— *mimēsis*—of a technical creature that is still impossible, but whose impossibility is covered up and compensated for by a play of illusion, a trick deployed for the sake of more astonishment. From the point of view of the history of technology, this mechanism occupies a peculiar time. The puppet lies on the border between two modalities and two epochs of conceiving and organizing *technē* and *mēchanē*. Let us say, by way of hypothesis, that this border is modernity itself, as a fleeting instant in which technology has not yet unfolded as a pure *operation* but still presents itself rather as *spectacle*.[16]

Benjamin offers an analogy: the transfer of the idea of this apparatus to philosophy. He thus proposes a *philosophical apparatus*. Doing this is, to a certain extent, putting philosophy in the perspective of an action and use, of an objective to be obtained: it is philosophy as *organ*. This inflection of philosophy could perhaps be connected to the contrast between interpretation and transformation that Marx proposed: the organic character of philosophy lies in the context of transformation. This character is motivated by analogical comparison. What is its key element? In other words, what does it mean to hide a theological dwarf in a puppet called "historical materialism"? Above all, what does it mean from the point of view of philosophy, of the modes of conceiving of philosophy that thus come together in this strange partnership? It could be said that, from this point of view, the apparatus that Benjamin proposes is also located on a borderline. Theology and historical materialism are two modalities and two epochs of thinking and practicing philosophy. They are such to the extent that both point to something common, to a fundamental problem they strive to clear up, with regard to which each one offers its respective organs of intelligibility: *history*.

The partnership of theology and materialism is strange. What is born of this alliance, what is thought *as* this alliance? Beyond the common object and common intention of theology and materialism, theology is relegated to an ancillary position, which, ironically, it turns around and denies. After all, it is theology that pulls the strings of the puppet, that ghost in the machine. What significance does theology's ancillary position have? What are the strings, what essential articulations of history require the intervention of theology, and of what kind of theology precisely? If we know that this is not a theology absorbed in the speculative contemplation of eternal divinity, but rather one that sinks deep into history and its "state of evasion," its *status deviationis*,[17] what is its core, the hidden lever it has in its power?

Benjamin's analogy includes another element that is not innocuous: chess. Just as everything in the game is a matter of triumph or defeat, the puppet always has to win, on condition that it takes theology in its service. Chess is a representation of war. In what war, and in the name of what should the puppet always win? We are not talking about a war for the representation of history, but about a war whose arena is history itself. The struggle for its (true) representation is of interest in war only to the extent that history is its sphere of activity. But the puppet, which certainly has to be articulated in accordance with a representation of history whose key is theological, always has to win in the war that *is* history. In view of this polemological conception of history, the efficacy demanded of the puppet is also the corroboration of its configuration as a technical mechanism.

By means of the chess metaphor, Benjamin's text inscribes history as a field of battle. But the battle is not carried out without a price: while inscribing history, the text necessarily inscribes itself into history, into its polemological tension. A similar inversion imposes conditions on reading. We cannot read Benjamin's postulate on the invincible force of historical materialism as if it were only a hypothesis whose validity is given immanently by the discourse in which it is formulated. For the same inscription of history, a certain radical rupture of discursive immanence has inevitably been produced. The figure of the puppet cannot be considered as if it were limited to being the rhetorical artifice that permits the investiture of a particular pretense, which at this point would be of interest only as a museum piece. It is the very truth value of this text and, with this value, the standards of its legibility that remain subjected to the polemological destiny of this pretense. In fact the puppet now lies on the ground, disarticulated and dismembered, showing all over the rudimentary quality of its skeleton and flesh and its clumsy, carnivalesque aesthetics. A multitude of statues that, in their time, were raised on pedestals, as inveterate expressions of a will to make history and its meaning endure once and for all, have been thrown down and shattered. They appear as so many other shreds of the puppet, whose invincible force someone attempted to contemplate in these fragments. What remains of him is, at most, his name. But Benjamin conjures him up precisely *as a name*, putting him under the shelter of quotation marks. They *say* distance. They bring something—an expression, for example—from far off, marking their remoteness as a trace of their provenance. Like picture frames, they separate the word from its surroundings. Applied to a name, they work like a prophylactic: they put it in quarantine, either so that it doesn't contaminate the medium in which it is imbedded or so that the medium doesn't contaminate it. In this way they preserve and reserve it, for example for some kind of operation. In a very plausible way, they function here in this guise, (p) reserving the name "historical materialism" for a secret operation, which the text will have to undertake in what comes next: the alliance with theology that I mentioned—and I mean with a certain theology. This is *the operation of citing*, which unfolds in a temporality proper to it. The "concept of history," for which we are trying to find the epistemological grounds, is constituted essentially by this operation.

The puppet lies on the ground, like a demolished statue. Its name lives on, and can be made present for us only when clamped between the pair of prophylactic jaws that are the quotation marks. And the hunchbacked dwarf? Does theology continue to need concealment, out of modesty or out of a care for its exhibition? Might it not be that we are attending today to a particular inversion of the link that Benjamin was proposing? Of course, historical materialism is something that should not let itself be seen; on the contrary, theology occupies the entire scene. However, this is not about a theology of history but about a theology of the end of history. By this I refer not only to what circulates as an explicit ideology of that end, but also to a general *tone* that modulates the discourses in which one attempts to measure the relation of our present to history itself. This tone has displaced the dominant tone that was the distinctive mark of modern discourse: the *critical* tone, which reached one of its peaks in historical materialism. The new tone—the "post-" or "after-" tone, if you will—is not, however, acritical or anticritical; it does not oppose the older one but guards it incorporated and controlled within itself. We could even say that the condition of its own possibility is this controlled incorporation. For this reason, this "post-" tone could be described as the tone of *administration*. Thus the "end of history" obviously does not mean that nothing more will happen. It means that all that could happen will still be administered and, even more (this would be the quintessential administrative postulate), that it can be administered in advance. The end of history is not its end, plain and simple (a concept according to which the end is still a divinity that might be experienced), but *the administration of history as something that touches its end*. In this sense, the theology of the end of history is an administrative theology. Its tone is not—nor can it be—apocalyptic for the very reason that it does not assume that nothing more can be revealed. Instead it assumes that everything that can be revealed, or that can be experienced, will be capable of being inscribed in the regime of administration. Of course, this is a theology that does not require God, unless he would find his place in a kind of sterile borderland, undaunted and always elusive, that it calls "the end." It offers instead an immanent double of providence in the figure of administration: in fact "providence" is the defining trait of the knowledge that belongs to administration.

Even so, what I have said requires caution. It seems, after all, that all thinking of history is necessarily, at the same time, a thinking of the end of history. That is, thinking history is to project its intelligibility. The intelligibility of something rests in the property that it can be contained by thought, as an object or theme. This "being contained" presupposes, as a condition of intelligibility, an apprehension of limits, the limits of that which one attempts to think—or else, in a limit case, the limits of thinking out with regard to that which is thought. The limit of history is its end. Thinking history, projecting its intelligibility, determining its meaning, is to think its limit simultaneously, in an explicit or tacit way. That is, to think the end of history. Indeed, this does not mean that thinking the end of history would be to *know it*, to have, for example, a *vision* or a present *experience* of the end. The end of history is not present in an immediate way in history, that is, it is not *available* in every one of the presents of history or in any one of them. This non-presence of the end in history can be conceived of in this first way: the end of history is transcendent to history itself. The end suppresses history, abolishing its specific temporality. *Knowledge* of the transcendent end is apocalyptic for this very reason: a brief glimmer is offered, by virtue of which the end makes itself ecstatically present in the present, as its image.

Against this attitude, a Kantian hurdle is raised, in the general context of the critique of *Schwärmerei*—fanatical exaltation that expects to *see* beyond the limits of experience. In Kant, the concept of history remains, *as a concept*, circumscribed within the limits of a reason that knows its limits. That is, Kantian reason remains in the dark about the *purpose* inscribed in its *origin*, but it can be aware of the *task* inscribed in its *structure*. This is why the Kantian thought of history is also a thought of the end of history, conceivable as the task of the realization of reason *in* history.

On the basis of this awareness, this task and plan for a rational expansion in history, another type of knowledge of the end of history can be articulated, one that is distinct from the apocalyptic type. By contrast, it does not require the ecstatic irruption of the end into the present of vision; rather it *measures* every present as a *step* in approaching the end, in other words as a step in the attainment of the end *in* history. Therefore one expects to have knowledge of it insofar as it would be present as a continual tendency in each of the presents of history, like so many other steps in the realization of rationality. The end that is conceived of here is not, of course, the suppression of history but the consummation of the task that unfolds in history.

Benjamin's text also attempts to think, in a certain sense, the end of history. What is important is the peculiarity of this thinking, which does not coincide either with the apocalyptic mode or with the progressive mode. Meanwhile the question of the end appears here under the name "happiness." This word names the end of individual history (biography) and the end of "universal" history. Certainly happiness is the notion of an end, more precisely a *lived end*, an end that *invites* one to live it. The scope of such an invitation is given by our expectations, by our hope. The latter takes on here the body of an *image of experience*, in other words it perceives its object in an image.

Is there hope without an image? Why can hope, in general, make images of that which is hoped for? Would this modality not be the one that feeds on hope, that maintains itself as hope? In any case, *maintaining oneself* belongs to hope. We ought to ask whether a failure to be realized might belong to hope in an essential way; this disappointment is the test that constantly pushes it to the brink of desperation, on whose edge it should maintain itself. Where hope does not find satisfaction, it has to maintain itself by anticipating what is hoped for. And, rightly, it is this anticipation that, as a fundamental trait of hope, has the character of the image—provided that we understand the image as a *promise of presence*, a representation that not only limits itself to replacing what is lacking, to compensating us and consoling us for the lack, but also promises that thing, giving us a first glimpse or, better yet, a *pledge of presence*. We should understand the image as a pledge of presence. Another might be (or perhaps especially is) the name, in which the image itself is erased.

But if hope perceives its object in an image of experience, Benjamin understands that only a certain *past possibility* seems capable of providing it, that this pledge of presence is determined by what is past. With this, he establishes the epistemological project that the theses intend to discuss and circumscribe on a paradoxical basis. We can approach the sense of this fundamental paradox by saying that it is not just an issue of guiding an explanation of the concept of history through the more or less banal recognition of an efficacy of the past over and against the present. It is instead a matter of a *determination of the presentness of the present through the past*. This determination opens in the present a difference that constitutes it, and in this way it cuts open the present itself.

Certainly the word "hope" hardly appears in the text of the theses.[18] It is difficult to represent its meaning without considering its relation to envy, which is made to refer to a distinct mode of dispossession. That is not a mode that remains tense in the anticipation of an instant of possible plenitude yearned for, but a privation that has taken place and in which desire finds cause for sadness only because of the patent impossibility of recuperating what would have satisfied it. Furthermore, it could be said not only that envy concerns *something* that we would have enjoyed living or having, but also that it is a late awakening of one's own desire. Envy would be defined as a preterition, not only of the object of desire but of desire itself. Hence its sadness. In a different way, the temporal dimension that opens up hope is the future: if hope keeps making us anticipate what is lacking even in the danger of its total disappearance, and precisely there, its fundamental reference is to the future. In a conception of history that evaluates its possibility of incorporating the perspective of hope, the future is the place of the end and of happiness—both at once. As for the possibility that the future might be designated and sketched out as such a place, on this depends the possibility of history (individual and collective) not closing in on itself; and this means closing in on a given present. We will see what significance this closure can come to have. However, Benjamin does not construct his inquiry around the privilege of the future, but around that of the past.

Even so, this privilege does not entail emptying out the future or shrinking its significance. For now, we could say that the significance that Benjamin concedes to the past allows him to keep the future open as a temporal dimension. Nevertheless, this process does not simply obey a conceptual strategy, as if the affirmation of the future in the opening of its possibilities were to require its own distinct comprehension of the past, and therefore only in this respect would the past become important. On the contrary, for Benjamin the dimension of the past determines all the time there is; it configures the temporality of time. The future—construed as a difference from the present, as a hiatus that opens up in the present, unresolved—comes not from some virtualities that would be lodged into the present and implicated in it, but from the past as something pending. The difference from the present from which the future *can* arise is the fissure that the pending past inscribes in the present. What is decisive in Benjamin's conception is that the past remains pending.

The past in a strict sense is the truncated past, the one that cannot—could not—be realized in its present. But precisely the aspect of the past that has been truncated is the index of its tension with respect to redemption. And this is based on a *"weak* messianic power" (GS I.2 694, SW IV 390).

Does this appeal not already announce the essential hermeneutic risk to which Benjamin's theory exposes itself? He had a clear awareness of the risk. In a letter from April 1940 that provides useful indications of Benjamin's self-understanding—a letter in which he tells Gretel Adorno about the manuscript—he says:

> The war and the constellation that brought it about led me to take down a few thoughts which I can say that I have kept with me, indeed kept from myself, for nigh on twenty years. ... I do not know to what extent reading it will surprise or even disconcert you—which I hope it will not. At any rate, I would like to draw your attention particularly to the 17th reflection; that is the one which should make apparent the hidden, yet conclusive connection between these observations and my previous works by offering concise information about the method of the latter. Furthermore, these reflections,

as much as their character is an experimental one, do not methodically serve the sole purpose of paving the way for a sequel to the "Baudelaire." They make me suspect that the problem of remembering (and of forgetting), which appears in them on another level, will continue to occupy me for a long time. I need hardly tell you that nothing could be further from my mind that the thought of publishing these notes (let alone in the form I am sending them to you). It would be a perfect recipe for enthusiastic misunderstanding.[19]

Precisely the messianism that the theses propose would be the pretext for this enthusiasm. Keeping it at bay surely depends on an exact understanding of the concept of "*weak messianic power.*" How could one not misunderstand it?[20] How could we distinguish and decipher this curious blend of criticism and fervor that seems to be its signature? Is it not constructed, in some way, as the philosophical apparatus that the first of the "theses" speaks about? The italics—which, otherwise, Benjamin has used sparingly—lead us to think of a secret, a hidden key to the power in question, a key that is called "weakness," just as the theological dwarf is the hidden cause for what the puppet of historical materialism accomplishes. But how can we think a power that, without ceasing to be a power, is weak? The meaning of Benjamin's concept seems to be based precisely on the indissociability of weakness and power.

Of course, the condition for understanding this concept, which is indiscernibly dual, consists in seeing to it that the power in question concerns the past. But this does not suffice. A power can relate to the past in many ways. It is the modality of this relationship that counts. To distinguish the modality that applies to weak power, the first requirement seems to be to contrast it with the type of power it implicitly opposes. Speaking of a weak power invites us to consider the notion of a strong power. We can suppose that both kinds might apply to the past. What distinguishes them? How does a strong power operate in relation to the past? It brings the past into the present. This bringing can take on a variety of forms, and tradition is the most general among them. Within this type of relation beats the heart of the will to refuse to accept the simple preterition of what has been [*lo sido*], but also a selectivity that receives from what is in the past precisely that in which the power of the present can be and wishes to be recognized. The strong power projects the present onto the past, like a beam of light that only outlines the profiles that correspond to the traits of the present. To the extent that it brings the past to the present in this way, a "strong power" is a present power—and it is the present of power. But the present of power is, as the operation of power, *domination*. A strong power is therefore a power that exerts dominion in the present and upon the present in which it is exerted. Its well-known verbal form is that of "*is*," which refers to dominion. Or, to put it another way, the signature of a strong power is marked by dominion. Its regime is the "is."

By contrast, a weak power is a power that accepts the past *insofar as* it is past. The simultaneous weakness and power rest on this acceptance: a weak power *welcomes* what has passed of the past [*lo pasado del pasado*], *receives* it (and, in proportion to this receptivity, is "weak"), and at the same time *resists* its investment (its capitalization) in the present (and, to this extent, is "power"). To resist this investment is to resist the strong power, the one that dominates precisely (in) the present. But the weak power is strong not only because it resists the strong power; and it is strong not in an (op)positional manner. Rather, it is strong mainly because it affirms (in the sense of accepting) the past as past. A play that we could call *evocative* is at work here, insofar as we understand that evocation is not the purely spontaneous act of conjuring up something already deceased but a hearkening to a *vocation* that calls from what is past ("the echo of dead voices"). If, as a power, the strong power presupposes the erasure of what has passed as past, the weak power does not erase (in other words, it does not disguise or cover up) the erasure that one day fell over what has passed and on account of which the latter was referred back to the shady realm of what has been [lo sido]—an erasure that does not cease to be reproduced: it does not erase it but rather highlights it.

It is as I pointed out before: the past as it properly is is the truncated past, that which *was not able* to be realized in its own present. The past that still preserves its validity today by virtue of the continuity of a dominant tradition is the modality in which the present takes possession of history through the figure of such a continuity. Consequently, Benjamin's most general philosophical project in these theses could be described as the introduction of *discontinuity* into history, for the purpose of validating the absolutely singular efficacy of the past qua past.

What is resisted in the figure of the strong power? What is the target of the critique that proposes that we think history from discontinuity? The text was written with polemical zeal, in order to influence the political consciousness of progressive forces.[21] Benjamin meant to take issue especially with the "progressivism" of those forces. The theses develop a critique of the ideology of progress. What he criticizes in this ideology is its anticipatory surrender in the face of the strong power. This surrender is backed by a representation of history that believes itself capable of perceiving a continuity in history (a necessity, a causal chain, a teleological *élan*), since continuity can belong only to domination. For this reason, the critique demands a different "concept of history." This concept must fracture the idea of continuity, which means that it has to fracture the matrix of continuity in which the concept itself gets purified.[22] Such a fracture amounts to a dismantling of the present as the dominant dimension of historical temporality. It should therefore manifest the fissure in the "is," where sovereignty encodes its historical enthronement. This fissure is the past. Thus the thematization of the past that Benjamin projects is not restricted to a critique of the idea of progress. Through the latter and within it, too, Benjamin attacks the foundation of the traditional conception of history, which underlies its various forms. Or, to put it another way, in order to dismantle the ideology of progress that ensnares the "progressive" forces, Benjamin perceived the need to dismantle the basic presupposition on which that ideology rests. This presupposition is *ontological*. In effect, the predominance of the present—under whose authority the reduction of the historicity of the historical takes place— has to do with a conception of being that keeps temporal difference within itself, under control, so to speak. For this conception, the "is" designates the (falsely happy) coincidence of being and time, the instant in which "is" coincides with itself at every point, signing its own identity. The theoretical format of such a coincidence is an *ontology of the present*.[23] But this coincidence is not random; it is not due to "naturalness," "mechanism," or the "spiritual" pulse of the movement of history. It is produced: the predominance of the present does nothing but express the violence of a domination that seeks to coincide with itself and to hypostasize itself in the present. This is why the coincidence in question presupposes the sustained, *continuous* intervention of a strong power, which unfolds as dominion. That the ontology of the present should be the adequate expression of a dominant force, in history and of history, reveals an ineradicable *political* element in its foundations, the element of a political *conflict*—that is, of a conflict of forces—that has the breadth of history as a whole. (Precisely this irreducibly conflictive element is what was encoded in the image of chess as a metaphor of war.) The object of attack that Benjamin's critique attempts to circumscribe in order to stir up the foundations on which the various "philosophies of history" are raised is, then, in its fullest dimension, a *political* ontology of the present.

Facticity

The epigraph from Nietzsche that presides over the twelfth thesis contests the *necessity* of historical knowledge, the *radical* necessity of *Historie* [the discipline of history]. In "Vom Nutzen und Nachtheil der Historie für das Leben" ("On the Use and Abuse of History for Life"), the young Nietzsche decided on this necessity from the point of view of life:

> we need it ... for the sake of life and action. ... We want to serve historiography only to the extent that it serves life: for it is possible to value the study of history to such a degree that life becomes stunted and degenerate—a phenomenon we are now forced to acknowledge, painful though this may be, in the face of certain striking symptoms of our age.[24]

It is what is pressing, what is painful about this necessity that interests Benjamin from the start. When and under what conditions does the knowledge of history become necessary, unavoidable? Undoubtedly, this is not a matter of "theoretical necessity" or "logical necessity" (like the need for coherence in historical knowledge, or for philosophical knowing to reach systematic completion). Rather it is about what is pressing, what is *urgent*. What concerns Benjamin is the necessity (*Notwendigkeit*) of a predicament (*Not*) in which, to put it one way, the time of history makes itself perceptible as such, in the syncope of its heartbeat. This "urgency" constitutes the subject of historical knowledge as the subject for which knowing history (and knowing it historically) is a question of life or death. And the "urgency" has consequences not only for the determination of this subject but also for the nature of knowledge itself. Urgency itself is the point at which the matter of the knowable irresistibly affects the proper form and intention of knowledge and the position and attitude of the subject. It is this feeling of urgency that moves Benjamin to engage in a polemic about the "concept of history."

In Benjamin's work, the same feeling excludes the intention of offering a new conception for the field of philosophy of history or a finished compendium of fundamental theses about it; and it rules out even more energetically the founding of a "historical science." After all, history as a science could be described as a "methodization" of memory. Benjamin's question addresses itself to the interest that governs such a methodization and that expresses itself in methodized memory. But this question is not a purely epistemological question, plain and simple. It is mainly a *political* question, which preconceives history as a conflictive field whose indelible stamp is the instance of suffering. Conditioned by this question, the reflections contained in the "Theses" are, in their full scope, epistemo-political. They propose a double critique, of the progressive and of the historicist conceptions. The critical zeal that stands out in them responds to the conviction about the powerful ideological efficacy of these conceptions, which bring along the unfortunate tendency to blind oneself about what is decisively at stake where they are concerned. Both maintain—one intrinsically, the other extrinsically—the historical obstacles that ensnare Marxism in the thought of the historical and in the problematic relationship it has with revolutionary action. As far as progressivism is concerned, these obstacles have been easy to perceive ever since the Second International. The decisive point of this combined critique lies in the fact that both visions come from the same matrix, which I already mentioned: the idea of continuity, the concept of a "homogeneous and empty time."

But in the whole scenario where this battle for the "concept of history" rages, Benjamin has not two, but three adversaries in view. Besides progressivism and historicism, there is also fascism. And it is absolutely decisive that he does not engage the third opponent at the same level as the other two, to which I will initially limit my remarks.

1. *Progressivism* is, so to speak, the figure of the introjected adversary, surreptitiously infiltrated behind its own lines, in its own spirit. This type of concept of history inspires "comrades," "fellow travelers," and keeps them safe from desperation and hopelessness, even in the midst of the most heartbreaking defeat, by making them trust the unfolding of an indispensable and ineluctably positive necessity in history. The "progressive" is an optimist through thick and thin, who refers the redemptive meaning of every setback and discomfort to the future, protecting her- or himself away from inclemency in this fashion. The theses were written, *above all*, in order to eradicate from the theoretical and political conscience of the "progressive forces" precisely this optimism about the future. *In opposition* to optimism, one should insist on the *irremissible* nature of what is past. To strive to justify the past, in its truncated condition, by a blessing or justice to come is ultimately to make oneself an accomplice of the forces that cancel the possibility of this arrival of the past, and at the same time to renounce the very possibility of thinking the historical.

But the debate with progressivism compromises not only the often utterly naïve pronouncements of social democrats, but also their distant presuppositions. The faith that animates these pronouncements has a long history, and the comforting sound of its tune, whether we want it to or not, eases the heart of the revolutionary in the end. The notion of progress is the core of a philosophy of history that presents itself as the secularized form of a theology of history. For the latter, which is represented in an exemplary way by Augustine of Hippo's monumental *De civitate Dei*, history is consummated, and for this reason it is distinct from nature, which is determined cyclically. It is consummated in salvation, which suppresses history, settling it into its transcendental meaning. This is why the subject of history is God. The concept of progress is therefore the secularized version of salvation, a version that presupposes humanity as the subject of history and inscribes the *telos* of history in itself. The concept of progress consolidates, then, *a teleological conception of history*. The epistemological key for this conception consists in slipping an a priori principle of historical development into a particular historical occurrence. This principle distinguishes what is knowable (the universal, the legal) from the insignificant or the expendable (the particular and the accidental). The immanent *telos* is conceived of as the full realization of this principle, whether it is actually supposed to be susceptible of being fulfilled or whether only an indefinite approximation to it is considered possible.

2. Historicism is the theoretical adversary of Benjamin's own intention to build the concept of history on the fragile, deferred and deferring efficacy of the past. It offers the paradigm of a conservative treatment of the past. In this sense, Benjamin aims at making evident the inauthenticity of this treatment; in other words he aims to show that it does not rescue the past *as past*. Instead historicism on the one hand tries to revive the past from a dominant interest in the present and, on the other, accumulates historical deeds in a homogeneous and empty time, making them capable of being capitalized in this way precisely for that interest. Its fundamental category is tradition, and it judges the historical process to be progressive decadence. Precisely this notion indicates the point at which historicism separates itself from progressivism, sharing with it the same matrix nonetheless. In contrast to the teleological universalism of the theory of progress, historicism wants to know the historic individualities (peoples,

nationalities, epochs, styles, institutions, personalities, etc.) without subsuming them under an a priori truth, which tends to erase precisely the truth of the particular within historical becoming. For historicism, each epoch is "immediate to God," and this means, as Ranke argued, that its significance, its "value," is not in what results from it, but in itself.[25] Therefore, in spite of its opposition to the teleological view of progress, historicism takes immanentization even farther. Against the Aristotelian interdiction, it offers itself as the "science of the individual" insofar as it intends to possess the epistemological key that gives access to historical individuality through the concept of (spiritual) *life* and in the *empathic* method. Historical knowledge is, then, conceived of as a process of penetrating into the past, which makes abstraction out of the temporal distance that separates the past from the present of its knowledge. Its epistemological ideal is to know the historical individuality better than it knew itself and to "revive" it in this way, that is, to justify it.

This empathic method is what Dilthey formalized philosophically in the experiential concept of understanding (*Verstehen*), which would establish the peculiarity and the epistemological originality of the *Geisteswissenschaften* (human sciences) in contrast to the natural sciences.[26] As much in historicism as in Dilthey, comprehension articulates a sphere of familiarity; it constructs a link of identity between the knower and what is known, a link that tends to suppress every moment of astonishment. These moments, however, would have to make themselves felt as soon as the knower recognized her- or himself as made possible and conditioned—together with knowledge—by the temporal difference that opens between the knower and the known. In this sense, we ought to refer to the ontological–hermeneutical corrective introduced in this concept by Gadamer, who was inspired by

Heidegger. Gadamer says that "the place between strangeness (*Fremdheit*) and familiarity (*Vertrautheit*) that a transmitted text has for us is that intermediate place (*das Zwischen*) between being an historically intended separate object and being part of a tradition. The true home of hermeneutics is in this intermediate area (*in diesem Zwischen*)."[27] The installation of comprehension within this "between" suggests the possibility of an irremissible loss, which constitutes not only what is known but the knowing subject, too, determining in the latter a moment of absence that cannot be reduced.[28]

Just such a loss is what historicism does not want to admit as the condition of its knowledge. And this very refusal, this same protective and self-protective gesture, is what makes it, in terms of a politics of knowledge, the conservative concept of history. From this point on, serious consequences follow for its own epistemological situation. If its purpose with respect to progressivism is to justify the historical individuality that progressivism tends to obliterate, it does this at the price of a reduplication of injustice: it, too, forgets that which the book on baroque drama calls "everything untimely, sorrowful, and miscarried that belongs to (history) from the start."[29] Thus it has been demonstrated that historicism does not deviate from the idea of universal history, but rather "culminates" in it (see Thesis XVII, GS I.2 702, SW IV 396)—except that it has to structure it on the basis of the relativity of multiple partial histories. Thus "its procedure is additive: it musters a mass of data to fill homogeneous, empty time." *Against this* it is necessary to insist on the *return* of what has been, which returns as irremissible.

The difference between one conception and another does not consist, therefore, in the desideratum of a universal history but in the way in which history is conceived of and projects itself. While the teleology of progress does it in a constructive way—and this means in a deductive way, on the basis of an a priori principle of historical unfolding—historicism proceeds by addition. This means that it proceeds inductively, from a plurality of historical individualities susceptible of being amassed into an empathic or comprehending knowledge. In the same way in which the epistemological truth of the theory of progress is idealism, the truth of the historicist conception is positivism. For both, the truth of history is not in itself historical but timeless, "eternal," whether it be located in the eternity of the past, as historicism is (see Thesis XVI, GS I.2 702, SW IV 396) or in the eternity of the future, as progressivism is. This means that neither of them has a critical concept of the present. For this reason, in spite of the variety of their intentions, ultimately they conspire to promote a vision of history that is based on identity and that stretches out, inevitably, as a "homogeneous and empty time." This, as I suggested before, implies an ontologization of the present, in accordance with which history's naturalization is consolidated, sealed with the idea of continuity. But continuity is possible only on the basis of forgetting what is truncated; and this forgetting, which is in no way "natural," is provoked and maintained by the power that dominates (in) the present. In this way neither progressivism nor historicism, as forms of historical knowledge, devotes itself to remembering. Instead, both are committed to forgetting; and when they forget, whether they want to do so or not, they secure their complicity with the dominators. Complicity is, then, a fundamental category in Benjamin's political epistemology. It is crucial to perceive the abyss on the edges of which this complicity prospers.

As an adversary, fascism is entirely distinct from the other two. It does not reach the same level, as I said. It installs something unprecedented: it does not propose a new concept of history, but rather relates to history as *factum brutum* of the present moment. If we could speak

of a concept of history that was consistent with it—
although Benjamin did not bother to elaborate it, because
it remained superfluous—that would be the concept of
(f)actualism. Or, put in a more economical way, fascism
reduces history to facticity. In this way it brings along
with it not the denial of inherited notions but precisely
the culmination of the continuist conception of history,
offering the absolute of domination. To it belongs the
vertiginous instant of the equivalence of power and being,
which only needs to be realized in order to show its crass
falsity, since an excess of power continues to be indispensable—as a *pathos* of annihilation—to sustaining that
equivalence. Thus is urgency determined. In order to take
stock of this, we need to understand facticity as the *limes*
of the historical.[30] Facticity designates, with an atrocious
exactitude, the point at which history is converted into
myth (into rigid nature). Fascism would be, then, the
program of the conversion of history into nature, encoded
in the (pre)potency of facticity, as a petrification of
historical happening and as the horrendous ecstasy of this
very petrification. Of course, such a conversion belongs to
the unfolding of any domain that seeks its legitimation by
purifying itself. But with fascism something arrives that
could perhaps be called the brute form of domination.
And in it the undesired truth of progressivism and historicism is portrayed, revealing them as neither conceptions
nor standards of intelligibility but as myths, emphatically
incapable of taking charge of this appearance.

In Thesis VIII, Benjamin says: "the current amazement
that the things we are experiencing are 'still' possible
in the twentieth century is *not* philosophical. This
amazement is not the beginning of knowledge—unless it
is the knowledge that the view of history which gives rise
to it is untenable" (GS 1.2 697, SW IV 392). Fascism is the
end of the philosophy of history. The stupor of the "angel
of history" is the emblem of this end; the angel knows
what is essential in history, the forever resumed unity of its

catastrophic movement. He also knows that, rigid as he is, he will not be able to fulfill the catastrophe. Overwhelmed with stupor, he still remains caught in the eolian trap of the astonishment that gave origin to philosophy of history.

In what precedes I mentioned, a bit in passing, what in truth constitutes the two dilemmas in relation to which the statute of all philosophy of history should in principle define itself. One is the theoretical problem of the knowledge of the individual. The other is the practical problem of the justification of evil and of pain. Historicism strives to give satisfaction to the first; progressivism dreams of resolving the second. But the former winds up reducing the brittle nature of historical singularity in the enraptured judgment of a superior memory. Meanwhile, the latter trusts the legality with which it plans to pay off the humiliating mortgage of the past, so that hypothetical future generations might be able to enjoy its yield. Truth and justice remain split. Under the pressure of fascism, Benjamin felt the onslaught of a thinking that thought the intersection of these two dilemmas and, from this inter-section, opened the possibility of thinking history and of thinking historically, beyond the epoch of the end of the philosophy of history.

Caracas, February 1993 and Santiago,
November 1995

3

Narration and Justice

Preamble

Among the plentiful works of the twentieth century devoted to narrative theory, Walter Benjamin's "The Storyteller" occupies a solitary place. The great schools— psychoanalysis, Russian formalism, phenomenology, existentialism, New Criticism, structuralist narratology, theory inspired by analytic philosophy, deconstruction, poststructuralism, postmodernism, feminism, theories of race—have each in turn dominated the scenes of debate.

It is certain that one main topic of "The Storyteller" is the difference between novelist and storyteller, to which Benjamin returned again and again, motivated by what he called his "old preference" for the latter.[1] But from this we can already gather that the theory of genres holds no interest for Benjamin. Since the essay concentrates on the figure of the storyteller, what is at issue is not the storyteller's product or the corresponding taxonomical problem. Storytelling is understood here as a social praxis, which goes along with a disposition, and what interests Benjamin is, essentially, not so much its aesthetic quality as its ethical significance.

Thus the main thing is what Benjamin proposes in this essay, the basic question he formulates. This is because the question cannot be simply accommodated in the field of literary studies, no matter how relevant the relationships in which he locates narrative might be for the conceptual evaluation of its structure and operations.

This question is oriented above all by the question of experience, and the latter, in turn, is subjected to a tension that pays heed, so to speak, to the nerve center of the entire essay. One pole of this tension announces itself immediately: it is the destruction of experience as a result of the unfolding, in modernity, of technology that culminates in war. The opposite pole is more reserved; it can be deduced from the chain of unanswered questions that the thesis of destruction must necessarily engender. For one, does technological modernity, in its link to the artisanal mode of production, lay waste to a type of experience per se? Or does Benjamin indicate that experience qua experience perishes? And, if this is the case, what is it that the destruction of experience is doing away with? In the end, what is this thing we call "experience," and what is its essential mark?

The development of the argument in "The Storyteller" offers convincing proof, I believe, that Benjamin considers the process of destruction compendiously. It is not a type of experience, but rather experience itself that is devastated by this process. But with this devastation something that belongs to the core of experience itself seems to get irremissibly lost, something that artisanal storytelling continues to protect like a dear treasure, something that is not substantive in itself but has the subtlety of a disposition, of fortitude and care, of attentiveness (*Aufmerksamkeit*).[2] This something is the vocation of justice that inspires storytelling.

The relationship between storytelling and experience is the matrix of Benjamin's essay, and vocation is what magnetizes it. Because of this, storytelling is not considered on the basis of its condition as an autonomous literary object, as most of the schools listed above look at it. It is treated instead as a case where the catastrophe of experience in the modern world can be examined in an exemplary way. However, this does not mean that story-telling becomes a subordinate theme, functioning as mere illustration. On the contrary, from Benjamin's point of view, precisely this matrix allows us to acquire a rigorous notion of what is essentially at stake in the practice of storytelling. And perhaps also in experience.

The Catastrophe of Experience

"The Storyteller" has hardly begun when we are confronted with two radical facts: the end of the art of storytelling and the crisis of experience. There is an inherent relationship between the two. The art of storytelling is the skilled exercise of a faculty that will have been constitutive to human beings since before anyone can remember: "the ability to share experiences" (GS II.2 439, SW III 143). A third fact comes to authenticate this sketch: as proof of the loss of this faculty, Benjamin calls attention to the muteness of the soldiers who returned from the Great War.

Benjamin had already warned about this in the essay "Experience and Poverty" ("Erfahrung und Armut"), which was probably written around 1933. There are only small differences in emphasis, although his intentions were different. In the most important of the differences, he speaks about the war, not war in general, as *that* confla-gration, one of "the most monstruous (*ungeheuersten*) experiences in the history of the world" (GS II.1 214, SW II 731, modified). In a certain sense, then, the war that was supposed to end all wars appeared in Benjamin's eyes as the experience that sealed the crisis of all experience. In this same text, with the intention of giving an account of the relationship mentioned in the title, he refers this

unexpected event to the reign of technology and to
its devastating consequences on individual and social
attempts to construct and configure experience.

> With this tremendous development of technology (*mit dieser
> ungeheuren Entfaltung der Technik*), a completely new
> poverty has descended on mankind. And the reverse side
> of this poverty is the oppressive wealth of ideas that has
> been spread among people, or rather has swamped them
> entirely—ideas that have come with the revival of astrology
> and the wisdom of yoga, Christian Science and chiromancy,
> vegetarianism and gnosis, scholasticism and spiritualism.
> For this is not a genuine revival but a galvanization. ... But
> here [Benjamin has just referred to James Ensor's paintings
> and their carnivalesque masquerade] we can see quite clearly
> that our poverty of experience is just a part of that larger
> poverty that has once again acquired a face—a face of the
> same sharpness and precision as that of a beggar in the
> Middle Ages. For what is the value of all our culture if it
> is divorced from experience? Where it all leads when that
> experience is simulated or obtained by underhanded means
> is something that has become clear to us from the horrific
> mishmash of styles and ideologies produced during the last
> century—too clear for us not to think it a matter of honesty
> to declare our bankruptcy. Indeed (let's admit it), our poverty
> of experience is not merely poverty on the personal level, but
> poverty of human experience in general. Hence a new kind of
> barbarism. (GS II.1 214, SW II 732)

Several things are important to emphasize about Benjamin's
argument. I would like to underline one in particular; and,
if it does not follow the letter of the text, I believe one
can gather it without committing the error of overinter-
pretation. In any case, Benjamin does not limit himself to
recording a transformation in the ways in which human
experience is realized—a transformation due to large-scale
historical disturbances. Nor does he speak in any proper
sense of a mere factic shock to the content of truth of
common and communal experience.[3] No. The historical

factum to which Benjamin refers carries along with it a transcendental effect: it is the very *possibility* of experience that remains in question, in a radical way. The transformations at issue take away from experience its conditions of truth, participation, belonging, and identity, all of which determine it as experience. In just this way might we understand the assertion that in muteness is revealed a complete "denial" of the experiences that give subjects a place and an orientation in the world. If "experiences" are the mode in which the existent relates to the truths of existence, the "denial" of the former implies a structural crisis. Consequently, war is not an event in a chain of events, no matter how great a significance one might give it. It is not an incident in a meaningful series (which goes by the name of history). Rather, it is the subversion of the meaning of history itself. A symptom of this perspective is the application of the term *ungeheuer* ("monstruous, violent, terrible, uncanny") to war as well as to technology, and to World War I because it was a technological war. This designation indicates that war itself is conceived of as the occurrence of something unusual in every respect, that is, as the advent of the empire of technology.

But, while on the one hand *this* event is not one among others, on the other hand it also seems valid to say that Benjamin does not limit his observation to the communicability of experience, as if that were a process extrinsic to it. On the contrary, as I understand it, his thought presupposes that this communicability is essential to experience and that a fracture in the latter is equivalent to a fracture in the former. To say it more precisely: what Benjamin calls "communicability (*Mitteilbarkeit*) of experience" does not refer to modes or processes of equivalence or universal homologation of experiences (in agreement with determinate cultural "universes"), but rather to forms of participation in a common experience. However, this experience is not preconstituted but *becomes common* in and through communication. To put it another way,

more formally, subjects constitute themselves intersub-
jectively, in the constant exposition to otherness. This
intersubjectivity is possible only in and through communication, and consequently this communication is essentially
an exchange of stories. All experience is, in this sense,
common. From the point of view of the concept of storytelling that Benjamin develops, this "becoming common"
is configured by two moments: that of experiences that are
shared through storytelling and its content; and that of
experiences that are shared by listening in common.

The end of the art of storytelling and the catastrophe of
experience: this core of Benjamin's argument is what allows
us to confront, with precision, the judgment that Hegel
had pronounced more than a century before. Although
this might happen without being stated, Benjamin's
discussion maintains a close link to Hegel's idea of "the
end of art." In Hegel, one could see a transition to a new
form of historical experience, for spirit only, insofar as one
laid claim to a different type of configuration and appropriation of experience; the "end of art" means that, as
an essential source of art, fantasy could no longer satisfy
truth.

What is this experience, and what is the experience that
determines the present moment, from which the "end of
art" receives its sanction? As Hegel formulates it in the
Introduction to Lectures on Aesthetics, the fundamental
index of the "present" is the complexity of relationships
that constituted the modern world, a complexity that
imposes everywhere the work of mediation.[4] Yet the issue
is not complexity as a given, but as a result of the fact that
the world itself takes on more and more the quality of a
construction accomplished through diligent and patient
human agency. The world as human work displaces the
work of art as reflection of the world: this would be the
meaning that modernity has for Hegel. Hence, the only
way in which it might be possible to take charge of this
complexity is to assume the concrete realization of this

world as a historical space for the fulfillment of freedom; and this is the same means that lies at the basis of the progressive construction of freedom, that is, the full development of *reflection*. In a general sense, "reflection" can refer to the mode of production of the modern world itself, whose original experience would have to be from now on reflexive, not reflected.

What distinguishes Benjamin from Hegel in *theoretical* terms is Marx's materialist reinterpretation of mediation, according to which we may only speak (figuratively) of a mediation of work, provided that we understand that this mediation really acquires its meaning in the modern context only as a universal system of production. This has consequences for the proper conception of art, as Marx already spelled it out in his reflections on this issue.[5] By developing Marx's rough ideas in an original way, Benjamin came to think that it was both possible and necessary to approach the development of art from the angle of transformations in the modes and media of production, insofar as these condition and affect the changes that occur in artistic creation. He proposed, then, the establishment of a historical and systematic relationship between the becoming of technique and that of art, in order to make the latter comprehensible from a materialist perspective that would be free of ideological debts.

But precisely the unrestricted capacities and technical accomplishments of mediation (to which Benjamin, in his celebrated essay on the work of art, refers as "technical reproducibility," that is, as a mode of production based on reproduction) bring along an essential transformation for the experience of the spirit, in such a way that this experience can no longer be construed as a space of reappropriation of spirit through the process of reflection. It can no longer be processed and served as the substance of the metaphysical subject's identity. Now the subject's experience can be described only as the experience of a loss; and this is not just the loss of an attribute or property. Rather it is the loss of the self and, furthermore, the experience of mourning for this loss, formulated in Benjamin's terms as the evanescence of the aura.

This evanescence itself is what marks the historical situation that Benjamin refers to under the description "the end of the art of storytelling." It assumes the closure of an atavistic mode of transmission of experience, based on artisanal production.

The Melancholic Difference between Technology and Artisanship

Clearly, Benjamin's discussion seeks to relate the organic principles of storytelling to a determinate social formation and mode of production. The artisanal mode and the type of society that it conditions are essentially linked in the forms and practices of storytelling. Nevertheless, the essay does not go deeper into the sociological elements of this linkage; what stands out is the temporal structure proper to it. This structure marks the importance of the experience of boredom, which could well be called the zero degree of experience. Certainly translations of *Langeweile* by *aburrimiento* (from Latin *abhorrere*, "to shrink back from," "have an aversion for/ be averse to," "disagree with," "differ from," "be inconsistent") or "boredom" (with its roots in the boring action of a drill or auger) lose sight of the temporal dimension that the German term encapsulates in its meaning: a "long while," if you will, the time in which one attends to nothing at all—because nothing stands out in the passage of the "while" and one only feels time, not its passing, as an empty expansion.

In Benjamin's appeal to this notion (see section 8 of "The Storyteller"), boredom is dignified with the title of the highest state of spiritual relaxation—a disposition in which one might find oneself while immersed in some humble mechanical activity such as spinning or weaving, a state of forgetfulness of self. It is as if these activities absorbed the passing of time in the rhythm of routine, allowing the feeling of that emptiness to be a condition of receptivity—"the gift for listening attentively"—that opens without reserve to the power of storytelling. It is as if self-forgetting were in turn a condition that favored the memory of storytelling and of what is told. In the end, it is as if, in this state that I called the zero degree of experience, the unemployment of the soul effectuated by employment in manual labor cleared a time for experience itself. "Boredom," Benjamin says in the key pronouncement of this chapter, "is the dream bird that hatches the egg of experience."

In a certain sense, the emptying out of time in boredom, which hands us over to time's in-difference, turns back to eternity, of which we will have occasion to speak.[6]

Centered on the interest of the subject and on the imperative of urgency and actuality, hyperactive modernity spoils this triple condition irretrievably, and modernity dissolves the community woven on the basis of it.

But what stands out in particular among the traits that typify modernity is the technical manipulation of nature in its entire extension, including human beings. The essential reference of storytelling to a form of life molded by artisanal work emphasizes the difference between two worlds—the world that gives it a context at the same time as it expresses itself in it, and the world configured by technical operations—in such a way that, from the start, it seems to betray a deep nostalgia. For readers of the great essay "The Work of Art in the Age of Technological Reproducibility," this cannot but surprise and even disorient, especially if we take into account that the two essays are more or less contemporaneous.

"The Work of Art" is guided by the recognition of a radical transformation in the status of the work as an effect of reproductive techniques: the transformation is such that reproducibility is now the primary condition and regime

of the work's production. This transformation brings
about a crisis in the traditional definition of the work, a
crisis regarding its originality as much as its connections
within the continuum of the tradition and, in the end, the
authority based on them. Ultimately, the work's aesthetic
condition also determines its reception and replaces its
ancient function for worship, but at the same time the work
retains secret links to its former character, which remains
fundamentally compromised by the transformation. And,
to the extent that technological media are responsible for
this epochal disturbance, it should be understood that
the artisanal mode of production, which is displaced by
the media, fundamentally contributes to that aesthetic
condition. Even more, Benjamin gives his diagnosis with
expressly political goals in mind, assuming that the regime
of reproducibility not only offers an occasion to formulate
a materialist theory of art but also favors the revolutionary
socialization of art through the elaboration of categories
that are useless from a reactionary standpoint. The reader
will remember the emphatic conclusion of the essay,
according to which the aestheticization of politics that
fascism promoted is countered by communism's politici-
zation of art.

In the section on what he calls "aura," Benjamin sums
up everything that defines the inherited status of the
work and that reproducibility consequently dismantles.
Of course, "aura" is one of the most celebrated words
in his repertoire. The essential difficulty of interpreting
it need not be stated again. "Aura" names a concept of
a dialectical nature. In general, what ought to be said
first is that an aura maintains its validity as long as it
does not belong to objects of perception and experience
but rather is their condition. The appearance of the aura
coincides, then, with its deterioration; the possibility of
thematizing it is at one with its critique.[7] Even though
the term does not occur in "The Storyteller," the concept
is present throughout.[8] While in several places it lingers

on the very idea of an "end of the art of storytelling," it is perhaps at the end of section 4 that the dialectical nature I referred to earlier is expressed most clearly. There Benjamin speaks of the end as "a concomitant of the secular productive forces of history—a symptom that has quite gradually removed narrative from the realm of living speech and at the same time is making it possible to find a new beauty in what is vanishing" (GS II.2 442, SW III 146). It would be problematic, then, if we failed to understand that storytelling has an aural character. Considering the discussion that I recalled above, "The Storyteller" expresses a hint of nostalgia and deep melancholy, evokes the inveterate artisanship of the tale, and, especially, reflects on the effects of technology on the storyteller's trade, its effects, and its contents. In these respects, it seems to locate itself at an extreme remove from that other celebrated essay.[9]

So storytelling and the novel are distinguished and counterposed here as artisanship and technology: storytelling, which has its basis in an artisanal society, is, Benjamin says, "an artisanal form of communication" in which the storyteller leaves her or his mark as the potter does on the vessel she or he molds. To the contrary, the novel's makeup betrays its belonging to the technological age. If it is still not, properly speaking, a technological form of communication, it is inevitably conditioned by the relationships that structure this new era, and it reflects the tensions and contradictions of the subject immersed in these relationships. The explanation of the birth of the novel relates it back to the invention of printing and, with it, to the manufacture of books. In a sense that comes close to what he says in the essay about the work of art, the novel is no longer a story to be shared among members of a community, but is produced with the express purpose of becoming a book. It is no longer something that forms part of common property but rather becomes available for individual consumption.

A crucial aspect of this transformation is the rupture with the oral tradition on which storytelling depends: the novel is essentially intended to be a book and, accordingly, withdraws decisively from oral transmission, which remains absorbed in the existence of a community. Communication mediated by technology goes along with the opening of a fundamental distance from experience, which novelists can no longer stamp with a particular, paradigmatic character. They have lost that very special type of certainty that is born alongside genuine experience. It does not rear up above experience, to look at it from the pinnacle of universality. It is not certainty about the concept, but rather about the knowledge—with the fragility of the witness—that something has happened, that something has taken place, even though it might not know exactly what or where and, in order to figure it out, might need to open a path through the murky thicket of language, looking there for faded trail markers. This certainty knows about the event. Radically uncertain, the novel signals the perplexity of the subject—the isolated individual—in the midst of the abundance of existence.[10]

As we can deduce from these notes, Benjamin does not work out a specific meaning for technical conditioning. Certainly, technologically mediated writing is from now on the basic format for the circulation of all narrative, and its essential effect is to uproot experience and to weaken communication. It could be said that silent and solitary readers make up for the impoverishment of their experience and for the loss of a communication that not only fails to provide elements for the conduct of life but, further, delivers like a mirror the image of their own shaky state of agitation—and does so with aesthetic delight in the work, just as when a spectator is seized by the aural relationship.[11]

But the uprooting is properly consummated with the new form of communication that information imposes. The press as a written medium carries technological mediation to an extreme in which the serialization and the indifferent universality encapsulated in the invention of the printing press are brought to fulfillment. Journalistic information homogenizes all content of experience, concentrating it and at the same time distributing it in minute particles of rapidly perishable news. For Benjamin, the point is its reliance on explanation, to which is entrusted the establishment of a new type of narrative truthfulness: the plausibility of what is transmitted. Information does not aim to provide elements of orientation in the world, as counsel does, by appealing to the freedom of the other when it takes into account the element of willingness to receive advice just as much as when it considers the use that might be made of that guidance in the situation at hand. Instead, information intends to provide tools for the homologation of situations and for the eventual manipulation of these tools according to programmed guidelines whose menu is contained *in nuce* in the explanation. The matrix of information is not pragmatic but cognitive.

Considering how relevant Benjamin's summary analysis of informative communication might be, on the one hand it could be said that its arrangement in a series defined by the radical crisis of experience—in which the novel is also situated—may not do justice to the specificity of the novel precisely with respect to experience. The implicit correlation between the pairs storytelling and praxis, novel and aesthetic delight, information and knowledge does not allow us to think of the multiple possibilities that the novel continues to bear within itself. On the other hand, the idea of a radical crisis of experience, conditioned to a great extent by the link between experience and the substance of tradition, does not allow us to think of alternative forms of experience either.[12]

Death as Sanction

A moment ago, when I spoke of the difference between artisanship and technology, I called attention to the dimension of time. Benjamin's reflections about information's inversion of experience not only encourage an interpretation oriented around an essential change of the discursive paradigm and its criteria for validity; they should also be understood in their reference to the question of temporality. Benjamin quotes Villemesant, the director of *Le Figaro*, according to whom the newspaper reader is more interested in that "which supplies a handle for what is nearest" (GS II.2 444, SW III 146), while news from afar gets lost beyond the horizon of what is considered prominent. This view emphasizes a profound change in the spatial dimensions of experience, which relates to what Benjamin regularly diagnoses as a general effect of technology, as it concentrates on processes of approximation and distance shortening. But, as journalistic information clearly shows, accompanying this effect is also a substantive modification of the temporality of experience: the time of information is the urgent and fleeting present, the moment of interest in the news; and this is a present that we know by the name of current events [*la actualidad*]. Of interest is only up-to-date [*actual*] information—what appears and expands decisively in the moment of its circulation, only to be immediately displaced by new information. All this of course presupposes a production of current events that is at the same time an inducement to interest. In this sense, the news item is much less its content than its flashing up in the circuit of information; and, if I may say so, it is more oriented toward in-forming the receiving subjects and defining their interest than toward providing elements that serve for guidance in life or for orientation in the world. From a temporal point of view, a news item is nothing but its characteristic of being current [*su actualidad*]: ephemeral in itself (or, in any case, provided with a duration that the production of the characteristic of being current regulates), it remains suspended over the general system of information—the only thing that is constant in the proper sense. But this constancy levels the differences between news items, making them all commensurable according to the interest that the system confers. Along with reinforcing the tendency essentially to blur the very texture of experience as perception and participation in what distinguishes different events (a texture without which they cannot be called events, strictly speaking), the constancy of news does the exact opposite of storytelling— which Benjamin associates with eternity, especially in "Notes on the Novel and Storytelling."[13]

The truth, if one goes spontaneously about it, is that Benjamin seems to be right when he speaks of this value of eternity: all genuine storytelling is, so to speak, surrounded by a halo of archaism, as if it were about a story that has been and will be told throughout time forever. And it could already be said that this is the criterion that allows us to recognize genuine storytelling and what Benjamin calls "the great storyteller." The aural character of narration is defined to a great extent by this peculiar modality, which is also responsible for the fact that the story that is told has a special, more or less anonymous character; one could call this the shadow of anonymity that can be glimpsed behind the signature of the great storyteller.

Benjamin also speaks of eternity in "The Storyteller," in a brief reference to a quotation from Valéry; it is, at once, a thought that gets its meaning primarily from the fact of death and a thought that disappears progressively from the consciousness of bourgeois society, in a process that is one with the loss of the communicability of experience and the end of the art of storytelling. One should not underestimate the importance of this statement in the complex argumentative economy of the essay. That evanescence, Benjamin insists, cannot be explained by

an acute change "in the face of death"—a change that
consists on the one hand in the systematic concealment of
this very face, its withdrawal from the collective gaze, and
on the other hand, in a way that is essentially linked to this
concealment, in what we could call the privatization of
dying. This transformation of how human beings relate to
death—the death of others and their own—should perhaps
be assumed to be the key to understanding what is definitively at stake in Benjamin's valorization of storytelling.

"Death is the sanction for everything that the storyteller can tell (*Der Tod ist die Sanktion von allem, was der
Erzähler berichten kann*)" (GS II.2 450, SW III 151). This
sentence, printed at the beginning of the eleventh section,
falls almost exactly in the middle of the essay. This merely
quantitative reckoning can be suggestive. In a certain
way, the sentence is like a hinge in the text. If we avoid
examining its content, the sententious tone itself gives it
a special weight. If we pay attention to what is said, this
weight increases. What does it mean that death should be
a sanction?

A sanction is the confirmation or approval of a law, act,
or custom. It has, for that very reason, a solemn character
and an authoritative scope. It is with this intention that
Benjamin conceives of death as the source of storytelling's
authority, a source that storytelling itself does not exhaust.
Storytelling takes this authority on loan, from death. This
leaves a completely unique imprint on the aural character
of storytelling, if I am to use a term I have used before (in
a somewhat hesitant way, that's true). Its mark is unique
in that it cannot be explained simply by its ideological
construction. Instead, one must refer to what can be
described as the foundation of communication, and thus
also the foundation of community.

Benjamin exercises a right when he assigns to death
the characteristic of a sanction comparable to what the
storyteller narrates. Exercising a similar right, we could
say that death is the aporia of narration, since it marks

the absolute limit of language, the constitutive possibility of silence.[14] This idea is important because it also points to another moment of differentiation between narration and novel, an essential moment from which he will later draw consequences. A distinction between death (*Tod*) and dying (*Sterben*) seems to be in order here. After all, readers of novels should be certain to attend to the death of the character they read about in order to decipher in it the "meaning of life" (I will return to this point), and they remain propelled the whole time toward the end of the novel. Meanwhile, storytelling attends to the hushed question that comes from dying, and attends to it as its most original element. This is the question of the unforget-table (*das Unvergeßliche*).

The concept of the unforgettable was introduced by Benjamin in the prologue to his 1923 translations of Baudelaire's *Tableaux parisiens*, on the basis of a paradox that has a theological edge. As he says in "The Task of the Translator," "one might speak ... of an unforgettable life or moment even if all men had forgotten it. If the nature of such a life or moment required that it be unforgotten, that predicate would imply not a falsehood but merely a claim unfulfilled by men, and probably also a reference to a realm in which it *is* fulfilled: God's remembrance (*Gedenken*)" (GS IV.1 10, SW I 254). In the present context, it would be appropriate to think that storytelling concedes a resonant space to the unforgettable, without naming it (because its essence remains untouchable to all human languages and because naming would have to be indistinguishable here from forgetting). This resonant space resists the end and closure in which the possibility of the novel might seem to lie, as if only the asymptotic and never empirically totalizable totality of stories could do justice to the demand that *is* the unforgettable.

But there is more to this invocation of the authority of death and dying. The relationship of this other aspect with the aspect I have just indicated could still not be adequately visible, and it will be necessary to wait for subsequent developments to make it more perceptible.

When he glosses on his assertion about death as sanction, Benjamin says that the storyteller's stories "refer back to natural history." He illustrates this view with an allusion to a story by Hebel, certainly a precious piece, called "Unexpected Reunion." I will still have to account for Benjamin's concept of "natural history," which is highly complex and does not always have the same meaning in each instance of its use in a variety of works.

In any case, it is a concept that belongs to the core of Benjamin's philosophy of history. It already featured prominently in *Origin of the German Trauerspiel*. From the point of view of his philosophy, one primary concern is to bring questioning—an insistent form of it—to bear on the matrix that conceives of history in linear, causal terms (this questioning will culminate in the "Theses on the Philosophy of History" of 1940) and that finds itself impaired, as a result, in the effort to embrace singularity and historical repetition in one single thought.[15] The point of this questioning is to place the connections between historical events in an ethical perspective (without forgetting the theological and political components that feed into them). In this effort, the distinction between human history (or world history) and natural history that the matrix presupposes should become essentially problematic.[16]

In line with this problematic character, and as the evocation of Hebel's story suggests, the storyteller reinscribes human history into natural history, appealing to death as the instance, the place, the event in which the two encounter each other in an absolute and unresolved way.[17] This reinscription is a sort of regression and, if you wish or will, a *repetition* of the "origin," which reigns as such only in and by repetition. Precisely this is what the storyteller's vocation of justice is all about.

Memory and Temporality

Regarding the background of the relationships and differences between human history and natural history, Benjamin stresses the forms of historiography, the chronicle, and storytelling. The contrast of the last two with the first should be especially illuminating. In fact, it reveals the essential kinship between the storyteller and the chronicler, to the point that the latter can be called "the storyteller of history." We have, for this reason, the testimonial presence of storytellers (and chroniclers) in their stories, free from the pretensions of objectivity that characterize a historiography that aspires to be a rigorous science. On account of this, we should also mention "conciseness" and the omission of explanations, detailed or not, and of psychological inquiries; all these would belong to "genuine narration," as we see in the story of the Egyptian king Psammenitus, told by the first storyteller of history, Herodotus.[18] The model that Benjamin has in mind most often in this context is the medieval chroniclers who, with the grand mural of soteriological history at their disposal, were able to dispense with the need to explain, that is, to apply the matrix of linear causality that I mentioned before. In exchange for that, chroniclers interpret, they link together the events that they relate "in the great, inscrutable course of the world" (GS II.2 452, SW 3 153). In comparison to this model, the storyteller might appear to be a chronicler of profane history for whom the course of the world is also impenetrable, whether in its capacity as a history of salvation or as natural history.[19]

In turn, the historian, the storyteller, and the chronicler are related to dimensions of memory. But the treatment of the latter is intended expressly for insistence, from a new angle of vision, on the difference between storytelling and the novel as epic forms. Benjamin's thesis, which adjudicates to the novel the mnemonic matrix of recollection (*Eingedenken*), has this precise goal. The first sign that points in this direction is the difference between the single and the multiple: recollection, as the element that inspires the novel, is oriented toward the unity of a life, an action, a character. It thus aspires to permanence. Memory (*Gedächtnis*) is the element of storytelling, it remains magnetized by the multiplicity of events, and it is ephemeral. While both, according to Benjamin, have their common origin in memory (*Erinnerung*), which inspires the epic in general, the novel alone would be possible by virtue of the essential separation of these two dimensions belonging to it.

It is not easy, after making exceptions for this case, to resist the temptation to discern certain traits that go by the name of recollection and to define epic or dramatic *mnēmē* ["memory"] in Aristotelian manner. This is due not only to the idea of a unity that belongs to their object. Aristotle says that a tragedy or an epic poem is *one* not because it chooses an individual as its topic, nor because it refers to the life of a single individual, which is inevitably composed of a variety of incidents that do not form a unity. Instead, Aristotle says, its subject matter is the unique action unfolded in the structure and the coherent sequence of its moments.[20] It is due, I insist, not only to this idea of unity, but also to that which should constitute its very substance. This is the meaning of the approving judgment that Benjamin devotes to the explanation contained in the *Theory of the Novel* by Georg Lukács, who conceives of the novel as the only literary form that has time as a constitutive principle. Its primary condition is the split between the factic becoming of life in time and meaning as a transcendental ideality. Seen in this way, the novel is defined structurally by the meaning of life, as the unity that ultimately measures its consistency.

This calls attention to the teleological character of the novel, which is propelled essentially to the paradoxical locus of its conclusion, just like the Aristotelian comprehension

of the unity of the fable, which has its defining foundation
in the memorable intelligibility of the totality of action. But
I say "paradoxical" because, in this place where definitive
certainty about the "meaning of life" in a novel should be
reached, we only have a glimpse of it, its fleeting shadow.
Benjamin argues that the essential difference between
novel and storytelling can be gathered from this novelistic
interest in the meaning of life on the one hand and the
narrative interest in offering a "moral to the story" on the
other—that is, of offering a lesson that can be invested in
the guidance or understanding of one's own existence. Both
novel and storytelling are conceived of as conclusive forms
of a different diegetic type. But, perhaps more decisively,
he confronts both, on the one hand with the will for
closure or for an end, if I may put it this way—a will that
drives novelists and their readers; and on the other with the
interminable character of storytelling. The right to ask, at
the conclusion of a story, "What happened next?" cannot
be abolished by the story. While in the novel death is not
only the seal, but the condition of life's meaning—which
nevertheless shows itself to be evasive in recollection—in
the art of storytelling death is the instance of an unfath-
omable memory. While in the novel the will for closure
rhymes definitively with the end of the art of storytelling,
in storytelling—and already in its most ancient beginnings,
when "art" had not matured yet—the desire of infinite
continuity prevails in the ideal plot of all stories. Because
this is perhaps an essential difference between one and the
other form: the difference between *will* and *desire*.

However (and this is the meaning of the paradox of
the conclusion that I spoke about), a narrative "then" lies
in the equally paradoxical locus of the beginning of all
storytelling; and it does so not only because it is prolonged
but also because it is anticipated by an "and then?" that
governs both the repetition and what is interminable in all
storytelling. This "then" remains present in the novel too,
in spite of the latter's will to closure.[21]

Natural History, Myth and Something Else about Memory and Narration

The magic of storytelling responds to an urge to continue: not simply to achieve continuity, but to renew. This is because it is something like magic that, in the primordial scenes of a story, keeps people united around the story-teller, whose voice—as one of the early drafts says—hardly emerges from the shadows. And it is the persistence of this ancestral magic that continues to hold the power to gather listeners together around many types of storytelling throughout their historical development. We already know the prominence that Benjamin gives to this communal power of storytelling, a power that, in its most refined figure, also defines the original popularity of storytelling, that is, its rootedness in the people. This, Benjamin suggests in section 16, is the magic of the fairy tale[22] that the child endorses when persistently asking, "and then?" This question does not stop even when confronted by the empire of death.

I was saying that death is the instance of an absolute and unresolved encounter, incapable of resolution, between human history and natural history. As we know, *Origin of the German Trauerspiel* designates allegory as the form that expresses this instance. In one of the most often cited passages of the book, we read, on the subject of the relation and difference between symbol and allegory: "whereas in the symbol, with the sublimation of downfall, the transfigured countenance of nature reveals itself fleetingly in the light of salvation, in allegory there lies before the eyes of the observer the *facies hippocratica* of history as petrified primal landscape" (GS I.1 343, O 174). In effect, natural history—as "the primal history of meaning or intention" (GS I.1 342, O 173)—is the essential fracture of history as a history of meaning (and certainly the inherited concept of history seems inseparable from the demand for meaning): a fracture imposed with the opacity of what we call "thing." As Eric Santner proposes, "natural history is born out of the dual possibilities that life can persist beyond the death of the symbolic forms that gave it meaning and that symbolic forms can persist beyond the death of the form of life that gave them human vitality."[23] This is also the essence of ruin, which, in its enigma, inexpressively signifies radical resistance to all symbolization, to all production of meaning, even as, in its silence, it demands them.

But storytelling is different from allegory, which invokes that fracture in a significant way, giving an account of "the experience of irremediable exposure to the violence of history" and making good precisely the repetition of the violence that destroys sense as a rhythm of the "natural."[24] By virtue of its own repetitive operation, storytelling practices a magic that evokes the first awakening of the human from the narcotic lethargy of its merely natural origin, where it was still "in harmony with nature," with the plurality of creatures. Natural history offers a different appearance, so that the magic of storytelling cannot be confused with a spell or incantation.

From this point of view, the notion of natural history intimately hosts a tension that opposes it in a decisive way to what Benjamin calls myth. If the essential vocation of Benjamin's thought is emancipatory, the issue is to undo the ties that bind human existence to the conditions imposed by its mythic constitution—to undo, that is, the demonic configuration of existence.[25] And one cannot simply believe that progress, the processes of secularization, and the very expansion of the technological management of human existence and of the world cancel out the demonic, with no possibility of its return. The demonic is recessive. Its burden continues to be effective and efficient where programs of rationalization and secularization seemed to have disenchanted the world. In its debate with these programs, Benjamin's plan implied a radical reformulation of the critique of reason, which expands the notion of experience, discovers rhetorical registers in the operations of reason that construct history, and formulates strategies in a dialectical key that can take charge of the complexity of the relationships that all this implies.[26]

In convolute N1, 4 in the *Arcades Project*, Benjamin says programmatically:

> To cultivate fields where, until now, only madness has reigned. Forge ahead with the whetted axe of reason, looking neither right nor left so as not to succumb to the horror that beckons from deep in the primeval forests. Every ground must at some point have been made arable by reason, must have been cleared of the undergrowth of delusion and myth. (GS V.1 570–571, A 457–458)

Delusion and myth chain the human being to the repetition of violence, while the terrifying face of nature looms everywhere. But "the liberating magic which the fairy tale has at its disposal does not bring nature into play in a mythical way, but points to its complicity with the liberated human being" (GS II.2 458, SW II 156, modified). As "The Task of the Translator" proposes with some complexity, translation points to the messianic horizon of pure language; storytelling, meanwhile, retains the memory of the first emancipation from mythic, demonic powers. The peculiarity of Benjamin's dialectic consists precisely in the installation in these two liminal moments, which accentuate the violence of the oppositions. This sharpening impedes the dialectic's ability to capitalize on oppositions in order to consolidate the identity that has made the differences its own, as constitutive and subordinate moments. Something completely other emerges in these boundary areas.

I have suggested that the aural character of storytelling is directly linked to one of its modalities, which not only gives an account of its appeal to the value of eternity, but also is responsible for this sort of strange anonymity it bestows on the story that is told. Benjamin refers to this point in introducing his reference to the story "The Alexandrite" by Leskov, which he reserved for the last of the chapters of his essay—a gesture that should be considered particularly significant. Speaking of the untarnished understanding that the storyteller—in this case in particular, the Russian writer—has of the world of the creature (and we will touch on this understanding and its relationship to justice before long), he celebrates this story as one in which "the voice of the anonymous storyteller, which existed before all literature," resounds in a fully perceptible manner. There are reasons to think that the "anonymous narrator," the narrator from before all literature and, I would say, also from before the *art* of storytelling, is none other than the "voice of nature"—as in the title of the story that Benjamin commented on in the previous section of "The Storyteller." The "story-teller's nature" is nature's storyteller, the storyteller of the world of the creature. Just as this "voice" operates in this story (we will recall that the source of storytelling is oral, and so is its proper nature)—that is, as a cause and occasion for remembrance—consummate story-telling, whose inspiration is the memory (*Gedächtnis*) that weaves the common ideal of all stories, is, so to speak, the catamnesis of the pure voice of that primordial narrator.[27]

Repetition

In a certain sense, it could be said that, in Benjamin, repetition is the supreme artifice. This is the significance that he gives it, all the way from *Origin of the German Trauerspiel* to "The Work of Art." In particular, repetition is the force that inexorably and tenaciously corrodes the aura. The definition of the latter is given in the great essay on the work of art: "an unrepeatable apparition of a distance, however near it may be (*einmalige Erscheinung einer Ferne, so nah sie sein mag*)" (GS I.2 478, SW IV 255, modified). It has its *sine qua non* in unrepeatability, in absolute and irreplaceable singularity (in being *einmalig*: something that happens once and for all, and only once).

But Benjamin's formula is carefully calibrated in its lexic and in its syntax, and demands to be read in all its phases and at various levels of truth, as it were. The word *Erscheinung* features in the formula "unrepeatable manifestation," meaning at the same time "apparition"— as in making something patent, *appearing*—and "illusion" or "trick"—said of something usually deficient, which merely *seems* to be in a certain way. As often happens in the grammar of Benjamin's concepts, these two meanings are connected in the same word and arranged in a reciprocal tension, which is dialectical in the sense that Benjamin gave this concept of tension and whose rule can be inferred only from constructions such as this one. In dialectics, each of two meanings reinforces the other to the extent that it contrasts with it, and this means that it constitutes it in and by opposition, but in such a way that each one makes the other manifest and is thus the principle of its critique. In fact we could say that the tension that remains in force between the two meanings makes explicit the essential ambivalence that the term *Schein* has in *Origin of the German Trauerspiel* or in "Goethe's *Elective Affinities*"; and that, as is well known, is the canonical definition of what the western metaphysical tradition considers to be the essence of beauty and the beautiful. The dialectic of these oppositions certainly takes a third thing into account, but its key lies in this third thing's being not the synthesis or reconciliation of opposites (in the constructive sense envisaged by Hegel and his followers). It is instead an interruption; Benjamin expresses this through the idea of "dialectic in suspense": *Dialektik im Stillstand*, which could also

be rendered "dialectic in a state of detention or arrest."
We can associate it with what the "Epistemo-Critical
Prologue" to *Origin of the German Trauerspiel* calls "the
death of intention" in relation to the possibility of truth
in its purity, and likewise in relation to the structure of
allegory and the messianic momentum and instant specific
to Benjamin's understanding of history. The third thing
is *not* susceptible to being coordinated with the terms
of the opposition in a categorial, logical, and epistemological manner but is precisely what that opposition
excludes. Thus one could say that this third, interruptive
thing—which flashes up, suspended between two terms in
opposition—is the destruction of the enchanted circle of
opposition. The interruptive third is, then, an excluded
middle, which destroys the plexus of the opposition in the
moment of its emergence. The destructive trait is inseparable from Benjamin's dialectics.

For this reason, the inability to be repeated cannot
be understood simply as an attribute that belongs to the
Erscheinung of particular objects by virtue of their special
nature. It should be grasped instead as an appearance
whose reason consists in the reiterative experience of
such objects under determinate and at the same time
surreptitious conditions, that is, conditions that do not
enter thematically in the circle of that experience. We will
recall that the concept of aura is associated with a thesis
about the conditioning and historical transformation of
perception. But at the same time the dialectic inherent in
Erscheinung not only reveals the illusion of a distancing
effect (in other words, an appearance of distance) that is
not receptive to any approach whatsoever. It also indicates
that this effect is the irreducible moment of truth of such
an appearance.

As a critical concept, aura is destructive. It attempts
to grasp the historical process and the productive forces
that cause the latent condition it designates to remain
exposed in their character and function. But, in line with

the idiosyncratic quality of Benjamin's dialectics, this does not mean only that the concept brings to light a condition that had remained historically valid and efficient even in its latency, sanctioning its epochal closure. We are dealing with a two-sided concept: if this concept looks to the end of the regime of determination of experience by the aura, it also looks to the tenacity of this regime, which encloses a remainder that critique does not exhaust. This tenacity certainly betrays itself in the reinstitution of the aura, a process that Benjamin recognizes in "The Work of Art" (e.g. in the creation of a star system in the film industry). But this is nothing more than the symptom of aural depth that resists all critique—an immemorial depth, if you will. Benjamin's use of the word "origin" takes account of it.

This depth is perhaps responsible for all the folds in Benjamin's conceptual apparatus. It can be considered both the inextinguishable remnant of magic and the indelible portent of redemption. It is the unforgettable. In Benjamin's essay, we can understand that the little story of Falun devised by Hebel—which contains an entire age of world history under its fragile wrapping and which, according to Benjamin, brings human history back to natural history—has its counterpart in the story of the alexandrite, where the inert stone, the last thing in the hierarchy of creatures and a paragon of muteness, is prophetic.

The storyteller makes the gesture of recuperating this depth, or inexhaustible remainder. The connection between this text and Benjamin's early reflections on language cannot be neglected. They continue to exert an influence on his mature thought. In "On Language as Such and on the Language of Man," Benjamin elaborates a theory of the name where one of the pivotal moments is, in his words, an "overnaming (*Überbenennung*) of things (of creatures) by human language."[28] The storyteller retraces this overnaming, restoring the creature to the language that suits it. In its most intimate gesture, storytelling would be the prophesy of the *return of the unforgettable*.

For this reason, repetition, too, can be conceived of simultaneously—not only as the supreme artifice but also as the rhythm of nature, as I tried to suggest earlier. While it can be said that the fundamental and structural paradox of storytelling (of all narration, in all its forms) lies in the fact that its task is the repetition of what is unrepeatable, the solution that is always resumed (and for this very reason is interminable) is the prophesy that storytelling presents, not in words, but in its gesture.

And, finally, while what is most striking from a programmatic point of view is that Benjamin attributes to storytelling (whose inveterate regimen—in other words aura—is undone by modernity) the very efficacy that he reserves in his thinking for the third term, this, as I argued above, is because the highest principle of this thinking is announced in this gesture: justice.

Storytelling and Justice

It has been said from the beginning. The statement that concludes the essay—"the storyteller is the figure in which the righteous man encounters himself (*Der Erzähler ist die Gestalt, in welcher der Gerechte sich selbst begegnet*)" (GS II.2 465, SW III 162)—indicates Benjamin's essential purpose.

Without harming Benjamin's intention to offer a substantive contribution to the theory of epic forms, "The Storyteller" is not, I insisted, an essay in literary theory. It does not set out to formulate the regulating principles of narrative; nor does it seek to contribute to a theory of genres. "The Storyteller" is, if I may put it this way, a fundamental essay in dicaeology, the theory of justice. Its defining theme is the connection it establishes between justice and storytelling. But the preparatory phrases for that closing statement—phrases that certainly lend argumentative credence to the idea—are perhaps not enough to calm what I suppose must be a feeling of astonishment in anyone who reads this climactic pronouncement—not without the help of an insistent interpretation. The sketch of the storyteller that precedes includes comments on the storyteller's gift ("the ability to relate his or her life," GS II.2 464, SW III 162, modified), on the storyteller's dignity (being about to tell "*all*" of it), on the resemblance of storytelling to the proverb and its exemplary substance, and on the benefits for life that accrue to anyone who pays attention and lends an ear; and these accrue not as the result of obeying an imperative but by virtue of friendly advice. Benjamin places great store by the meaning of these benefits for the spirit, just as he insists on the capacities of storytelling. All this can help us understand the concluding assertion, but does not completely suffice.

What that sentence means, I believe, demands that we ask about the meaning, the structure, the character of the connection that I mentioned: what justice can a story deliver? That the storyteller should be the figure in which the righteous person finds her- or himself is not due merely to the storyteller's psychological or ethical disposition, but to the very operation of storytelling, which necessarily has to be compared to how language (the substance of narration) can do justice. In his essay on Karl Kraus, Benjamin offers an important indication to this end, at the moment when he discusses the functioning of the quotation for the Austrian writer:

> In the quotation that both saves and punishes, language proves the matrix of justice (*Mater der Gerechtigkeit*). It summons the word by its name, wrenches it destructively from its context, but precisely thereby calls it back to its origin. It appears, now with rhyme and reason, sonorously, congruously, in the structure of a new text. As rhyme, it gathers the similar into its aura; as name, it stands alone and expressionless. In citation the two realms—of origin and destruction—justify themselves before language. And conversely, only where they

interpenetrate—in citation—is language consummated. In it is mirrored the angelic tongue in which all words, startled from the idyllic context of meaning, have become mottoes in the book of Creation. (GS II.1 363, SW II 454)

This sort of disjunctive synthesis of destruction and origin, presented here in the functioning of the quotation in Benjamin's interpretation of it, can serve as an orientation for the analysis of narrative justice; and it can point in two directions. On the one hand, there is the question of language itself. How, in what forms, and under what conditions is language—can it be—resistant to justice? Benjamin had given an answer to this question in the early "On Language as Such." That answer is what he describes as the bourgeois conception of language, which sanctions the general and generic speech of the entity of the sign, governed by exchange value. For this reason, it is also the sign's ability to be exchanged—its equivalence, so to speak, in the valuation of the linguistic marketplace, its essential principle in what has been said earlier about "overnaming"—that buries the precious jewel of the name under dense layers. All this would have to be set alongside this hostility toward justice. In place of it, against it, story-tellers—as I said—take language back to the time before overnaming. They do this without arrogating the power of the name for themselves; instead, they refer back to it in asymptotically. And they grant a primitive use value to language in the form of advice.

On the other hand, to make a point closely related to what was said before, storytelling gives an account of care for nature in the plurality of its expressions and manifestations; however, unlike nature, it is not itself destructive. The righteous character of storytelling consists in giving an account of the happening of the singular, that is, in giving an account of what is singular in its happening. It is perhaps the justice of the trivial; maybe this is why Benjamin accords such importance to detail and to the trivialities that characterize storytelling in the traditional sense and why he associates detail with the spirit of the chronicle. But the essential term that he uses in this context is "creature." Not just human beings (and the most eminent among them, the righteous person), not only living beings, but everything in nature, all along a hierarchy that ascends to the highest things and descends into the "abyss of the inanimate," whose principal example is the prophetic stone of Leskov's story. The human, the animal, the thing, are all creatures in their intimate singularity, which is at the same time their indelible alterity. Everything is a creature, on condition that it be perceived in its irreducible and unrepeatable singularity; and, for storytelling, this means on the condition of its being *repeated* in its irreducible and unrepeatable singularity.

Benjamin emphasizes that storytellers do justice to the creature, that they are not its avengers but its "advocates (*Fürsprecher*)." The justice of the story and of storytellers consists in the fact that they issue neither a judgement nor a legal ruling. In storytelling the creature is not judged; instead, it is given room to play—in the space of language—so that storytelling can make the irreplaceable traits of its individuality resonate. Benjamin's interest in stories of rascals and criminals must surely be related to this. More than a vindication of the outlaw, what we have here is the opening of a space in which the outlaw appears before or on the margins of any sentence.

For this reason, storytelling's justice is nothing but care for the creature, the fortitude of the righteous man that Benjamin reads in the celebration of the maternal *imago*, and for which he has an unequivocal name. The end of the second chapter of his essay on Kafka mentions it: "even if Kafka did not pray—and this we do not know—he still possessed in the highest degree what Malebranche called 'the natural prayer of the soul': attentiveness. And in this attentiveness he included all creatures, as saints include them in their prayers" (GS II.2 432, SW II 812).[29]

Envoi

"That truth is not an unveiling that destroys the mystery but a revelation that does it justice (*daß Wahrheit nicht Enthüllung ist, die das Geheimnis vernichtet, sondern Offenbarung, die ihm Gerecht wird*)," Benjamin declares in the "Epistemo-Critical Prologue" to *Origin of the German Trauerspiel* (GS I.1 211, O 7). As do so many other texts by Benjamin—so that we might even say that this is an indelible trait of his writing—this essay gives the impression of guarding a secret whose revelation would completely destroy the force of its truth. It is a weak power, then, like the one "The Concept of History" speaks about.[30] This weak power—which is the one and only one required for justice—might well be the power that weaves together both the story of the storyteller and Benjamin's text. It is as if what the essay itself—in its general fabric, in its argumentative vectors and its repertoire of images and its examples, its twists and turns, in short, in its style—says about storytelling gave an account of itself.

Santiago, 2008

Notes

Notes to Introduction

1 My epigraphs, in order, are from Bolívar Echeverría, *Ensayos Políticos*, ed. Fernando Tinajero (Quito: Ministerio de Coordinación de la Política y Gobiernos Autónomos Descentralizados, 2011), 210: *¿Pero estamos, en verdad, en medio de la realización del deber ser, como lo pretende el discurso histórico de los vencedores? ¿Si pasamos la mano sobre el relato bien peinado de esa historia, pero lo hacemos a contrapelo, como recomendaba Walter benjamin, no resultará, tal vez, que lo que ella tiene por "excepciones"—excepciones que no dejan de aparecer con fuerza incluso en nuestros días— puede enseñarnos más sobre la historia de la democracia en la modernidad, y sobre sus posibilidades actuales, que lo que ella reconoce como "regla"?* (in my translation); Walter Benjamin, "The Storyteller: Reflections on the Works of Nikolai Leskov" [1936], trans. Harry Zohn, in *Illuminations* (New York: Harcourt Brace Jovanovich 1968), 83; and Sebastián de Covarrubias, *Tesoro de la lenguua castellana, o española* (Madrid: Luis Sánchez, 1611): Cuento *se llama el puntal que se arrima a lo que amenaza ruina, y de alli se dixo andar, o*

estar en cuentos: estar en peligro, y sustentarse con artificio (in my translation).

2 "Benjamin in Latin America," ed. David Kelman, *Discourse* 32.1 (2010). Kelman's introduction follows Elissa Marder's work to "state that the survival of [Benjamin's] work depends on the *translation* of his biological life." To a greater or lesser degree, the essays in his volume endorse this understanding of Benjamin's reception in Latin America. See also Elissa Marder, "Walter Benjamin's Dream of Happiness," in *Walter Benjamin and the Arcades Project*, ed. Beatrice Hanssen (London: Continuum, 2006), 184–200. An early collective overview of Walter Benjamin's reception in Latin America can be found in Nicolás A. Casullo, Gabriela Massuh, and Silvia Fehrmann, *Sobre Walter Benjamin: vanguardias, historia, estética y literatura: una visión latinoamericana* (Buenos Aires: Alianza, 1993).

3 Michael Löwy's deep engagement with Benjamin's work centers on the "Theses on the Philosophy of History" (though his remarks on the theological strain in Benjamin's writing are crucial to understanding Löwy's own conceptualization of the theology of liberation in Brazil and elsewhere in Latin America). See especially Michael Löwy, *Fire Alarm: Reading Walter Benjamin's "On the Concept of History"* (London: Verso, 2005); Michael Löwy, "Reflexiones sobre América Latina a partir de Walter Benjamin," in Bolívar Echeverría, ed., *La mirada del ángel: En torno a las tesis sobre la historia de Walter Benjamin* (Mexico City: Facultad de Filosofía de la UNAM / Ediciones Era, 2005), 35–44; and Michael Löwy, "Marxismo e cristianismo na América Latina," *Lua Nova* 19 (1989): 5–22.

4 There has been so much recent work on Walter Benjamin published in Latin America that any list risks seeming grotesquely partial; when it is not over-long, it will be idiosyncratic. In addition to Löwy's work and the *Glosario Walter Benjamin: Conceptos y figuras*, ed. Esther Cohen (Mexico City: UNAM / Instituto de Investigaciones Filológicas, 2016), I have found especially valuable the following works: Elizabeth Collingwood-Selby, *Walter Benjamin: La lengua del exilio* (Santiago: ARCIS/LOM, 1997); Willy Thayer, *Technologies of Critique*, trans. John

Kraniauskas (New York: Fordham University Press, 2020). On translation, Pablo Oyarzun, "Sobre el concepto benjaminiano de traducción," in idem, *De lenguaje, historia y poder* (Santiago: Universidad de Chile, 2006), 153–195; Andrés Claro, "La traducción como 'posvida' histórica," in idem, *Las vasijas quebradas: Cuatro variaciones sobre "la tarea del traductor"* (Santiago: Ediciones Universidad Diego Portales, 2012), 639–661; Miguel Valderrama, *Traiciones de Walter Benjamin* (Adrogué, Buenos Aires: Ediciones La Cebra, 2015); and *Walter Benjamin, A tarefa do tradutor*, ed. Lucia Castello Branco (Belo Horizonte: Fale/UMFG, 2008). Centering on violence, Pablo Oyarzun, Carlos Pérez López, and Federico Rodríguez, eds., *Letal e incruenta: Walter Benjamin y la crítica de la violencia* (Santiago: LOM, 2017); Federico Galende, *Walter Benjamin y la destrucción* (Santiago de Chile: Ediciones Metales Pesados, 2009). On art, vanguardism and modernism, Nelly Richard, *The Insubordination of Signs: Political Change, Cultural Transformation, and Poetics of the Crisis*, trans. Alice A. Nelson and Silvia R. Tandeciarz (Durham, NC: Duke University Press, 2004); Macarena Ortúzar Vergara, "Estéticas del residuo en el Chile del postgolpe: Walter Benjamin y la escena de avanzada," *Acta Poetica* 28.1–2 (2007). Recent collections of essays include *Walter Benjamin: Fragmentos críticos*, ed. Esther Cohen, Elsa R. Brondo, Eugenio Santangelo and Marianela Santoveña (México City: Universidad Nacional Autónoma de México / Libros Malaletra), 2016.

5 On the "now-ness" of Benjamin's readings in the anglophone world, see Kevin McLaughlin, "Benjamin Now: Afterthoughts on the Arcades Project," *boundary 2* 30.1 (2003): 191–197. Project MUSE, muse.jhu.edu/article/41345.

6 For *Jetztzeit* in Latin America (and in Spanish), see the entry by Marianela Santoveña Rodríguez in *Glosario Walter Benjamin*, 229–239. A different way of approaching *Jetztzeit* can be found in Héctor Schmuckler, "La pérdida del aura: la nueva pobreza humana," in Casullo et al., *Sobre Walter Benjamin*, esp. 249–251.

7 See Elizabeth Collingwood-Selby on "experience" in Collingwood-Selby, *Walter Benjamin*, 9–10.

8 The modality of possibility in Benjamin is the subject of Samuel Weber, *Benjamin's -abilities* (Cambridge, MA: Harvard University Press, 2010).

9 "Salvador Allende: Letzte Ansprache an das Volk Chiles." http://www.kommunisten.ch/index.php?article_id=377.

10 This widely cited translation of Allende's last words was recently discussed by Fernando Muñoz León in his article "Competing Narratives about Sacrifice: Three Readings of the 11 September 1973 Coup in Chile and their Conflicting Constitutional Projections," *Political Theology* 17.6 (2016): 507–524.

11 The most compelling account I know in English of Benjamin's complex concept of justice is to be found in Peter Fenves, *The Messianic Reduction: Walter Benjamin and the Shape of Time* (Stanford, CA: Stanford University Press, 2011). Neither he nor Julia Ng, whose elegant entry "Gerechtigkeit" in *Glosario Walter Benjamin*, 105–117 offers a superb synopsis of the topic, address the matter of "doing" justice as Oyarzun understands it; neither articulates *Gerechtigkeit* with storytelling, though both attend to the relation between justice and translation.

12 I follow Judith Butler, *Giving an Account of Oneself* (New York: Fordham University Press, 2005), a work that, despite very seldom addressing Benjamin's work directly, turns on the articulation of justice and storytelling as doing that we find in "The Storyteller" and in Oyarzun's *Doing Justice*.

Notes to Prologue

1 [TN: Here and in the foregoing paragraph, Oyarzun's *que se haga justicia* is translated in various ways, to capture the varied meanings of the verbal construction. In note 3 I will address the use of the pronoun *se*, a Spanish resource with no equivalent in English that is used throughout this Prologue.]

2 [TN: "Capacity" translates *poder*, which can mean "power" but also is the modal verb corresponding to the English "can." Capacity therefore designates what is possible because the power exists for it to be accomplished. In the preceding

sentences Oyarzun has provided me with some elaborations on the relationship of justice to otherness that do not appear in the Spanish original.]

3 [TN: The original phrase in the Spanish text is *se hizo justicia* and Oyarzun is speaking about the pronoun *se*, which is emphasized graphically. This pronoun is sometimes called the impersonal or no-fault *se*. In English as in Spanish, the passive voice engenders some of the problems of responsibility discussed here, in that it obscures the identity of the agent that "does justice." Hence the translation transfers to the passive voice what the Spanish text attributes throughout to the word *se*. As the following discussion makes clear, however, the English construction's use of the past participle ("is done") suggests something finished or concluded, which the Spanish phrase—with its active, finite verb, *se hace*—lacks.]

4 [TN: In Spanish one may use the future tense forms of a verb to express a hypothetical possibility; thus *habrá justicia* would be translated "there might be justice," or even "there must be justice." But the Spanish future does not typically correspond to an English imperative, and this is emphasized in English through the substitution of "shall" for "will": "there shall be justice."]

5 [TN: The Spanish distinction between *la ley* and *el derecho* does not coincide exactly with the English difference between law and right, although it resembles the German distinction between *Gesetz* and *Recht*. In Spanish, study of the law, understood as concrete, codified laws and the abstract conceptions corresponding to them, is usually referred to as training in *derecho*, that is, in right or in (legally prescribed) rights. Although we often speak of human rights (*derechos humanos*) as the ground of justice, Oyarzun refers in what follows to Benjamin's insistence on the distinction and incompatibility between obeying the law and attaining justice. Depending on the context, I have translated *derecho* as "law," indicating the Spanish parenthetically when the context calls for another choice.]

6 It is not improbable that Benjamin was thinking of something like this when he wrote: "The law that is studied but no longer practiced is the gate to justice./ The gate to justice is study" (GS II.2 437, SW II 815, modified).

7 [TN: Speaking of minimal effects, Oyarzun refers here to the deployment of *se* within parentheses—*un (se) apenas audible*, "a barely audible effect of the passive voice"— suggesting that the word *se* is inessential. This expression cannot be matched in idiomatic English, since the meaning of the impersonal passive voice is sustained by the whole structure rather than by a single word.]

8 Obviously, I mean to evoke the title of Benjamin's early "On Language as Such and on the Language of Man" (GS II.2 140ff., SW I 62–72).

9 *Schatzkästlein des rheinischen Hausfreundes* (*The Treasure Chest of a Rhenish Family Friend*) is a collection of stories, almanac articles, and humorous anecdotes by Johann Peter Hebel (1760–1826), published for the first time in 1811, in Stuttgart, by J. G. Cotta.

10 Quoted in Jacobson, *Metaphysics of the Profane: The Political Theology of Walter Benjamin and Gershom Scholem* (New York: University of Columbia Press, 2003: 166 and 168, for the English and the German respectively).

11 Ibid.

Notes to Chapter 1

1 And this is true whether this "naturalness"—that is, the relationship of philosophy with natural languages—is interpreted negatively, in the sense of the transcendence of the intelligible, the idea, meaning, inexpressible in any language, elevated above the mechanisms of language, or whether it is understood positively, from an instrumental perspective, for example.

2 This is the situation that Aristotle assigns in the *Rhetoric* to the examination of saying itself, of "how one should speak" (*hōs dei epein*) as distinct from "what one ought to say" (*ha dei legein*): see *Rh.* 3.1, 1403^b. A bit later, at 1404^a, he also distinguishes it from "delivery," the art of the actor. [TN: The Greek text of Aristotle's *Rhetoric*, in the standard OCT edition of W. D. Ross, and an English version of it by J. H. Freeze can be found on the Perseus website.]

3 Here we should keep in mind that the essay I am commenting

upon premeditates the intimate identification of philosophy with the theory of language.

4 I am thinking of a particularly saucy episode of Gulliver's visit to the School of Languages at the Academy of Lagado: one of the projects debated there considers the abolition of words in favor of the immediate communication of things. Leaving aside the difficulty that this would bring to large and varied business dealings, the project, we are told, failed because of the obstinate resistance of women, the common masses, and the illiterate. See Jonathan Swift, *Gulliver's Travels* (Cambridge University Press, 2012): part III, chapter 5.

5 By making use of the documentation in Benjamin's correspondence, its editors, Tiedemann and Schweppenhäuser, date the first version, entitled "Lehre vom Ähnlichen" ("The Doctrine of the Similar"; GS II.1 204–210, SW II 694–698), to January 1933. The second version diverges from it in unmistakable ways. The later text, to which I refer, must have been written between July and September of the same year (see GS II.3 950 ff.). Irritating as this might seem, its consideration in the context of Benjamin's early reflections on language is based on the sometimes slightly enigmatic insistence of certain themes, motifs, and modes of analysis throughout Benjamin's trajectory, in spite of the radical changes that his thought might have undergone. This insistence has provoked more than a little bit of perplexity about the dating of some texts. In any case, we have the benefit of some of Gershom Scholem's observations regarding "The Doctrine of the Similar" that refer back to enthusiastic conversations he had with his friend Benjamin in 1918.

6 According to Aristotle, metaphorical talent consists in a perception of similarity (*to homoion theōrein*), and is inalienable and untransmissible. It is rooted in the very nature of the human being and therefore has an essential relationship with *logos* ["reason," "discourse," "speech"], but it also imprints on this human nature what could be considered the innermost core of what is specific to it. It would still be possible to argue that such an inalienable moment of the *logos* is irreducible to the universality of the

logos, that it is its condition and limit. See Aristotle, *Poetics* 22, 1459ª5ff.

7 The German word *Sprache* ties together the meanings of language in general and particular mother tongues. Thus, as it allows the transition from one to the other—from which some thinkers drew benefits, for example Hegel—it also shelters the tenacity of their difference. It seems to me that, in Benjamin's use of the term, one should pay attention to the insistence on particular languages, in spite of the reference to language in general. In this difference is inscribed the problem of translation. [TN: I have distinguished here between *lenguaje* "language" and *lenguas* "languages," using the plural to set the general concept apart from particular instances. In what follows, it is sometimes helpful to use the word "tongue" in the more idiomatic expression "mother tongue" to refer to a particular language (*lengua*), especially when Oyarzun evokes the notion of *un lenguaje sin lengua* "a language without mother tongue."]

8 Not a language without mother tongue [*un lenguaje sin lengua*], I insist—and this point is important when we come to evaluate the meaning of conventionalism. The latter sustained the specificity of language on condition of reducing the particularity (the local being, if you will) of specific languages. Such a reduction is indispensable to guarantee the idea of *universal mediation*, which can be considered to lie as the heart of all conventionalism. And let it be said emphatically that this crystalline quality does not dissolve in the regime of mediation. If we look at this from the point of view (noted earlier) of a "bourgeois conception of language" organized around the sign's deleterious ability to be exchanged, we can say, on the contrary, that a pure language is of a symbolic nature. Benjamin invokes the concept of the symbol toward the end of the essay I am discussing: "for language is in every case not only communication of the communicable, but also, at the same time, symbol of the noncommunicable" (GS II.1 156, SW I 74). The symbol will figure in Benjamin's thesis, a piece titled *Der Ursprung des deutschen Trauerspiels* (*The Origin of German Trauerspiel*), and will come into play in the text on the translator.

9 It seems decisive that, along with the irreducibility of being to language, Benjamin simultaneously seeks to secure the irreducibility of language to being—a theme that, by the way, circulates silently through the twists and turns of the essay and begins to resonate from the moment the law of the call becomes audible, that is, it becomes the call of the law. We are on the path that leads to this irreducibility. But, for language to be irreducible to being and indelible in it, languages must be irreducible to language. The theme of translation is already prefigured, it seems to me, in the concept of this irreducibility.

10 The concept of allegory is in the theoretical center of the book about German baroque drama, which I mentioned earlier. Of course, it constitutes one of the essential (and perhaps the most highly charged) categories in all of Walter Benjamin's reflections on language, literature, aesthetics, and history.

11 Particularly with the essential compromise that theories propose between the nomination of a thing and its cognition. I will return to this issue.

12 [TN: Antonomasia is the substitution of a proper name by an epithet considered characteristic to the person or entity designated by that name (e.g. "the Maid of Orléans" for Joan of Arc). It is, like many terms for rhetorical figures, an ancient Greek word—*antonomasia*, itself a derivative of *antonomazein*, "to call by a different name"— assimilated into modern languages such as English or Spanish. Spanish tends to use it in the phrase *por antonomasia* to refer to what is "quintessential" or to what is so and so "par excellence."]

13 Concerning the unrestricted eminence of the Law—the thinking of the Law—which I believe we can recognize in this text, it is worth remembering Benjamin's youthful interest in Talmudic studies and in the Kabbalah, as well as the special reception that Judaism receives in his entire oeuvre.

14 Here, too, there is an undeniable brush with mysticism, but there is also a difference from it in which philosophy finds its validity. This is not a matter of protecting elusion (such a protection inevitably leads from mysticism to mystification),

but rather one of watching it as one follows it on its path. This means that the name takes care of the elusive (what is named), pursuing it and watching out for its (re)integration into being. In a certain sense all human names are appellations (*Nachname*), but only to the extent that they are offered on the basis of an original pro-vocation (a *Vor-name*), which calls what is named (and elusive) into being. As far as the relationship between philosophy and mysticism goes, elusion cannot be a postulate of thinking, that is, its pretext; rather it must be renunciation (the acceptance of its finitude) as the gift of its supreme effort, its *task*.

15 It is a *weak* power, in the notable formulation of the second thesis in "On the Concept of History" (originally published in 1940). Allow me to quote the relevant passage: "The past carries with it a secret index by which it is referred to redemption. Doesn't a breath of the air that pervaded earlier days caress us as well? In the voices we hear, isn't there an echo of now silent ones? Don't the women we court have sisters they no longer recognize? If so, then there is a secret agreement between past generations and the present one. Then our coming was expected on the earth. Then, like every generation that preceded us, we have been endowed with a *weak* messianic power, a power on which the past has a claim" (GS I.2 693–694, SW IV 390). This "weak power" indicates acceptance of the past *qua past*, an acceptance that *receives* it and at the same time *resists* its investment in the present. Here we find *evocation* at work to such extent that we may understand that it is not a spontaneous act of conjuring up something expired but a hearkening to a *vocation* that calls from outside the past: it is "the echo of dead voices." On this, and in particular on the concept of "weak power," see the second essay in this volume, especially pp. 61–65 in this volume.

16 All the same, since poetry is the preferential linguistic form adopted in defending naturalism (as is the case in Vico, for example), discussing its translatability amounts to taking naturalism to the limit of what it can tolerate. In any case, I ought to emphasize that, in Benjamin's texts, the privilege of the poetic word is inseparable from the archetypal character of the sacred word. In consequence it is not just poetry, but

rather poetry and religion that form the matrix of Benjamin's meditation on translation: at stake there is the sacredness of the word and the word of sacredness.

17 After I had finished the greater part of this essay, I found a piece titled "Torres de Babel" (in French, "Des tours de Babel"), written in 1979 by Jacques Derrida and published almost a decade later, in 1987, in a journal from Seville called *Er*, in a Spanish translation by Carmen Olmedo and Patricio Peñalver (see Bibliography under Derrida). Its first part is devoted to a commentary on Benjamin's preface. Derrida's work travels various paths that I follow here, notably and primarily the question of law and that of the task.

18 One thing that should give us pause, even though dwelling on it requires more space than I have here, is Benjamin's anticipated resistance to what has spread in the last decades in the field of literary studies as "theory of reception"—a domain that derives its legitimacy from the philosophical framework of hermeneutics. I will state very briefly what, in my view, we can conjecture about it—and this relates to something I will say later about history. The relationship works with a type of relationship with history—as history of works and as history of effects (*Wirkungsgeschichte*)—a relationship that, in spite of circumstances, is ultimately constituted on the basis of a dominant transmission (on this, see my essay "Sentido, verdad, hermenéutica," in my collection *De lenguaje, historia y poder: Diez ensayos sobre filosofía contemporánea*, Teoría, 2006, pp. 23–76). To reception, Benjamin opposes rescue (*Rettung*)— the rescue that Habermas attempted to thematize in "Bewusstmachende oder rettende Kritik," in his *Kultur und Kritik* (Suhrkamp, 1973, pp. 302–344), as a non-traditional relationship with the historical; this would be a relationship that resists—in other words, remains passive to—the violent compression of the historical, on the picture plane of domination. This relationship with history also attends to what interrupts the continuity of domination. After all, history does not owe itself to domination but to the gift. And the gift that grounds the historical—an irruptive gift, a power switch [*interruptor*], a gift of death—cannot be received.

19 On Cratylus's statement, see *Cratylus* 436d ff. Socrates's thesis, which contains the presupposition of a kinship (*sungeneia*) of things themselves, is developed at 438d ff.

20 "The proper name is the community of the human being with the *creative* word of God," and "the theory of proper names is the theory of the frontier between finite and infinite language." A similar limit is signaled by knowledge, lack of which defines human language. And this lack creates a task that is not different from the translator's: "in a strict sense, no name ought (in its etymological meaning) to correspond to any person, for the proper name is the word of God in human sounds" (GS II.1 151–152, SW I 69, modified).

21 As he connects the name and the translation in an essential way (as I believe is necessary), Rolf Tiedemann (*Studien zur Philosophie Walter Benjamins*, Suhrkamp, 1973, p. 48) points out: "Just as 'all the great writers' of literature contain 'in between the lines their virtual translation' into other languages, phenomena also contain their names in a virtual way. Therefore, the alternative to convention or mimesis has become obsolete for the philosophy of language; Benjamin's theory of language responds to the latter with a theory of translation."

22 Let us say only in passing: space—and time—would be a multiple, irreducible song, without a key or score. Concerning this and the motif of the vessel, see H. Leivick's words that Harold Bloom makes into the epigraph to his *Kabbalah and Criticism* (Seabury Press, 1975, p. 7): "A song means filling a jug, and even more so breaking the jug. Breaking it apart. In the language of the Kabbalah we perhaps might call it: Broken Vessels."

23 See also my essay "Traición, tu nombre es mujer," in *Ver desde la mujer*, edited by Olga Grau, Ediciones La Morada, Editorial Cuarto Propio, 1992, pp. 143–156.

24 Franz Rosenzweig's seminal essay "Scripture and Luther" insists on this constitutive paradox of translation. Its German title is "Die Schrift und Luther" and it was written in 1926, only three years after Benjamin's preface to his versions of Baudelaire. The essential relationships, in affinity and difference, between these texts would require an extensive analysis, which I cannot undertake here. Rosenzweig also

considers the relationship between translation and speech and, furthermore, situates translation on the terrain of *Sprache*. He begins his own "task of the translator" precisely with what we could characterize as the recognition of the irreducible duplicity of this task, and thus with another variation on the theme of the implacable Italian proverb: "To translate means to serve two masters. It follows that no one can do it. But it follows also that it is, like everything that no one can do in theory, everyone's task (*jedermanns Aufgabe*) in practice. Everyone must translate, and everyone does" (Franz Rosenzweig, "Scripture and Luther," in Martin Buber and Franz Rosenzweig, *Scripture and Translation*, Indiana University Press, 1994, p. 47).

25 Without ground: where nothing can grow any longer. In a certain sense, this is the very condition of translation, which, "ironically, transplants the original into a more definitive linguistic realm, since it can no longer be displaced by a secondary rendering" (GS IV.1 15, SW I 258). Benjamin insists on translation's inability to be retranslated; this surely has something essential to do with the untranslatability that springs from translation itself. In the same way, it is not thematizable—untouchable—for the act or the gesture with which it is accomplished. The inability to be retranslated suggests that, ironically, the most definitive ground to which it brings the original has the completely fragile nature of a suspension over an abyss.

26 This, let me say in passing, means that translators—and we should remember that "The Task" focuses not on translation but on the figure of the translator—are subjects that satisfy the condition for speaking [*decir*] only to the extent that the condition that institutes them as subjects is retracted [*se desdice*]. The subject properly speaking would emerge only on the basis of a refusal to translate, by arrogating for her- or himself the origin of speaking, which would be possible only by way of a (self)concealment of the retraction [*desdecimiento*] that constitutes the subjects and sends them on their way. Therefore Benjamin's theory of translation would contain, as if in abbreviated form, a sort of genealogical theory of the subject that undermines the ground of its own emergence.

27 The English translation of the French original cited by Benjamin can be found in Stéphane Mallarmé, *Selected Poetry and Prose*, edited by Mary Ann Caws, New Directions, 1982, p. 75.

28 Quotation, then, as the quintessential relationship, historical and philosophical. Hannah Arendt has persuasively argued for this view in the third section ("The Pearl Diver") of her brilliant essay "Walter Benjamin: 1892–1940," in her collection *Men in Dark Times* (Harcourt, Brace, & World, 1970, pp. 153–206). To quote is to give care and assistance to the fragment, to that in history that runs the risk of getting lost. We recall here an assertion made in "On the Concept of History": "only for redeemed humanity is the past quotable in every one of its moments" (WN XIX 31). And it should not be overlooked that Benjamin conceived of his essential *work* as a system of quotations. The *Passagenwerk* is a work of passages, where the arcades rise up, as in the Paris beloved by Benjamin, as the key and primordial element of the translator (GS IV.1 18, SW I 260). The arcades are literally like words: in short, they let in the light, the intangible.

29 I tend to use this terminological distinction—translatability and translativity (*traducibilidad y traductividad*)—to express the difference between a restricted and an expansive notion of translation. The first continues to refer us at all times to an original, a model, a pre-textual text, or even to a posthumous intelligibility. The second suggests the indefinitely proliferating circulation of texts that absorbs in its play all possible reserve belonging to origins or ends. Therefore it is neither a pre-text nor post-text.

Notes to Chapter 2

1 This title does not originate with Benjamin, who limited himself to the more circumspect "On the Concept of History." Certainly Benjamin, who speaks of "notes" (*Aufzeichnungen*) and "reflections" (*Reflexionen*), also refers to them as "theses" in a letter to Max Horkheimer dated February 22, 1940: *Je viens d'achéver un certain nombre*

de thèses sur le concept de l'Histoire. This letter is quoted by Tiedemann and Schweppenhäuser at GS I.3 1225, from *Gesammelte Briefe* (Suhrkamp, 1995), vol. 6, pp. 399–401. See also *Werke und Nachlaß* (Suhrkamp, 2010), vol. 19, pp. 177–178 and 310. In short, there are important considerations that invite us to discard this title because it does not aspire to the status of philosophy that these very reflections ponder. Rather than an epitome of certain knowledge, the "theses" are a taking up of positions in struggle; they do not form a body that could be unequivocally called a "philosophy of history." I will have more to say about this in the last of these "suggestions."

2 The editors gave this section the title "On the Theory of Knowledge, Theory of Progress" (GS V.1 570 ff., A 458ff.).

3 Tiedemann and Schweppenhäuser argue convincingly, on the basis of Gershom Scholem's testimony, that the fragment must have been composed around 1920–1921 (see GS II.3 946–947). Adorno, who gave it the title by which it is now known, assumed that the date must have been 1938, when Benjamin read it to him.

4 See the great "Epistemo-Critical Prologue" to the *Origin of German Trauerspiel* (*Ursprung des deutschen Trauerspiels*, 1925): "Truth never enters into a relation, let alone an intentional one. The object of knowledge, an object determined in conceptual intention, is not truth. Truth is an intentionless being formed from ideas. The comportment appropriate to truth is therefore an entering and disappearing into it, not an intending in knowing. Truth is the death of intention" (GS I.1 216, O 12). The persistence of this idea in Benjamin can be exemplified by fragment N 3.1 from Convolute N in the *Arcades Work*, which is particularly important for what it says about the dialectical image in the theses: "Every present day is determined by the images that are synchronic with it: each 'now' is the now of a particular recognizability. In it, truth is charged to the bursting point with time. (This point of explosion, and nothing else, is the death of the *intentio*, which thus coincides with the birth of authentic historical time, the time of truth)" (GS V.1 578, A 462–463).

5 Kant is the theoretical axis of "The Program." Plato plays this role in the "Epistemo-Critical Prologue" to the *Origin*

of German Trauerspiel mentioned in note 4. A third name also echoes undeniably in the latter text: Leibniz, the great philosopher of rationalism, contributes the fundamental schema for the comprehension of the "idea" with his monadology, which, in the form of the notion of the "dialectical image," will continue to exercise a fascinating influence on the Benjamin of the theses. In each case, we are dealing with a lawful form of knowledge that is not constituted by extrapolation from what appears empirically. This could never give credit to truth in its being but, almost to the contrary, to a form that imprints itself on, or configures, the empirical. "Truth subsists (*besteht*) not as an intention or meaning that would find its determination through the empirical world but rather as the power that first stamps the essence of that world" (GS I.1 216, O 12). The difference implied here between the empirical and the experiential is essential for "The Program," as can be gathered from what follows.

6 In the word's debasement into the sign, the latter is understood as an abstract medium of exchange and equivalence, useful in the circulation of merchandise. This is the heart of what Benjamin calls "the bourgeois conception of language." See the first essay in this volume, especially pp. 5–6.

7 The question of history was certainly on the horizon of this early program. In a letter to Scholem sent on October 22, 1917 whose sequel was this very text, Benjamin states: "I believe I recognize the ultimate reason that led me to this topic, as well as much that is apropos and interesting: the ultimate metaphysical dignity of a philosophical view that truly intends to be canonical will always manifest itself most clearly in its confrontation with history; in other words, the specific relationship of a philosophy with the true doctrine will appear most clearly in the philosophy of history; for this is where the subject of the historical evolution of knowledge for which doctrine is the catalyst will have to appear" (Walter Benjamin, *Briefe*, edited by Gershom Scholem and Theodor W. Adorno, Suhrkamp, 1978, vol. 1, pp. 151–152; *The Correspondence of Walter Benjamin*, translated by Manfred R. Jacobson and Evelyn M. Jacobson, University of Chicago Press, 1994, p. 98). In the same letter he mentions the decision to write his dissertation on "Kant and history," which he did not complete.

8 Aristotle, *Metaphysics* A.1, 981ª15: ἡ μὲν ἐμπειρία τῶν καθ᾽ ἕκαστόν ἐστι γνῶσις.

9 Georg Wilhelm Friedrich Hegel, *Enzyklopädie der Philosophischen Wissenschaften im Grundrisse 1830: Werke*, edited by Eva Moldenhauer and Karl Markus Michel, Suhrkamp, 1986, vol. 8, p. 108 (§38). In English, *Hegel's Logic*, translated by William Wallace, Clarendon / Oxford University Press, 1975, p. 61.

10 Hegel, *Enzyklopädie*, p. 108; *Hegel's Logic*, p. 61, translation modified.

11 Hegel, *Enzyklopädie*, pp. 49–50 (§7); *Hegel's Logic*, pp. 10–11. For an elaboration on this reading of Hegel, see my essay "Un apunte sobre el concepto de experiencia en la *Enciclopedia* de Hegel," *Revista de Humanidades* 8–9 (2004): 139–145.

12 The etymological link between *Erfahrung* and *Gefahr* rests on the meaning of *fahren*, "to go on a trip." There is also an etymological link, in Spanish, between *experiencia* and *peligro* (danger) and, in English, between *experience* and *peril*—all of which can be traced back to *experiri* (to try) via *periculum* (danger).

13 "Intensive" does not mean "rich" or "motley" but, as I just said, "transformative [*alterador*]." Benjamin's reflections on experience would eventually have to be complemented by what he says in the 1933 essay "Experience and Poverty" ("Erfahrung und Armut") (GS II.1 213–219, SW II 731–735).

14 Here I am not thinking of the "religation" attached to the transcendence of an otherworldly divinity but rather to what one would have to call imminence: the vortex of the temporality of experience.

15 Both these passages (1.2 and 1.3) belong to Convolute K in the *Arcades Project*, whose title—*Das Passagen-Werk*—was chosen by its editors, as was the title of Convolute K, "[Dreamlike city... Jung]."

16 And, as we know, Benjamin was the thinker of the border, which was inscribed physiognomically in his indelible intellectual figure, biographically in his death, and theoretically in his conception of modernity.

17 Benjamin's "theology" is indeed one of a kind: it lacks the substantive and identical centrality of the divine and affirms

instead the pure eventuality of the messianic, the differential efficacy of its "coming." Let us recall, in this regard, the comments in note 14 of this essay.

18 See thesis VI: "The only historian capable of fanning the spark of hope in the past is the one who is firmly convinced that *even the dead* will not be safe from the enemy if he is victorious" (GS I.2 695, SW IV 391).

19 GS I.3 1223–1226. Cf. Gretel Adorno, Walter Benjamin, *Correspondence 1930–1940*, edited by Henri Lonitz and Christoph Gödde, translated by Wieland Hoban, Polity, 2008, p. 286.

20 Brecht notes in his *Journal*, with regard to his reading of the "theses" in August of 1941: "in short, the little treatise is clear and presents complex issues simply (...) and it is frightening to think how few people there are who are prepared even to misunderstand such a piece" (Bertold Brecht, *Arbeitsjournal* vol. 1, edited by Werner Hecht, Suhrkamp, 1973, p. 294, as quoted by Tiedemann and Schweppenhäuser in GS I.3 1228; cf. *Bertolt Brecht Journals*, translated by Hugh Rorrison, edited by John Willett, Methuen 1993, p. 159).

21 I will return to this point in the fourth "suggestion," "Facticity."

22 I suppose that Benjamin's recourse to the *image* should be connected to this. The irreducible singularity and temporality of what has been could not be apprehended in the concept, which conforms to its traditional determination. Roughly stated, the concept makes what is known present, while the image evokes it, recalls it.

23 This notion has been proposed by Reyes Mate in "La historia de los vencidos: Un ensayo de filosofía de la historia contra las ontologías del presente," in *Cuestiones epistemológicas: Materiales para una filosofía de la religion*, edited by J. Gómez Caffarena and J. M. Mardones, CSIC, Anthropos, 1992, pp. 183–207.

24 Friedrich Nietzsche, *Die Geburt der Tragödie: Unzeitgemäße Betrachtungen: Kritische Studienausgabe*, vol. 1, edited by Giorgio Colli and Mazzino Montinari, Deutscher Taschenbuch Verlag / de Gruyter, 1999, pp. 245–246; in English, Friedrich Nietzsche, *Untimely Meditations*, translated by R. J. Holling, Cambridge University Press, 1997, p. 59, modified.

25 [TN: This characterization of historicism appears in "On Progress in History": see Leopold Ranke, *Theory and Practice of History*, Routledge, 2011, p. 21.]

26 [TN: It is in his *Introduction to the Human Sciences* (Princeton University Press, 1989) that Dilthey distinguishes the particular character of understanding in the *Geisteswissenschaften*, with an eye to providing a theoretical foundation for the historical practices of his time.]

27 Hans-Georg Gadamer, *Wahrheit und Methode. Grundzüge einer philosophischen Hermeneutik*, J. C. B. Mohr (Paul Siebeck), 1990, p. 279; in English, Hans-Georg Gadamer, *Truth and Method*, Seabury Press, 1975, pp. 262–263.

28 Of course, it cannot be said that Gadamer takes into account the moment of this loss in its entire scope. His model continues to be recognition and pertinence; this undoubtedly makes them more acute, as a creative continuation of tradition, but validates them ultimately on the basis of an originary value of familiarity. "Astonishment" is conceived of here only in relation to the distancing and objectivizing procedure developed in natural sciences; it is not represented in the mind as a difference inherent in historical temporality itself.

29 See the passage already quoted from the *Origin of German Trauerspiel* (GS I.1 343, O 174). It is worth recalling that Hegel posited the need to take charge of this gaze, of this relationship of "affliction" and "mourning" (*Trauer*) with what has happened, in order to fix the point of departure of the philosophy of history. What this gaze has before it "in the history of the world (is) the concrete image of *evil* in its most fully developed form. If we consider the mass of individual happenings, history appears as a *butcher block* on which individuals and entire nations are immolated; we see all that is noblest and finest destroyed. No real gain appears to have been made, and only this or that ephemeral work lingers on, already bearing the mark of decay on its brow and soon to be supplanted by another as ephemeral as itself" (*Vorlesungen über die Philosophie der Geschichte*, vol. 1: *Die Vernunft in der Geschichte*, edited by Johannes Hoffmeister, Meiner, 1955, p. 261; in English, *Lectures on the Philosophy of World History: Introduction:*

Reason in History, translated by H. B. Nisbet, Cambridge University Press, 1975, p. 212, modified). Indeed, in Hegel this "mourning" is sublated by the sovereignly strong form of consolation that reason offers.

30 Benjamin understood that it is a pressing task of critical thinking to resist the spell of facticity. In a long letter about his work on Baudelaire sent to Theodor Adorno from Paris on December 9, 1938, he expresses—with consummate lucidity and in the form of a subtle observation about the philological temperament of a philological nature—the danger that threatens the kind of treatment of history that wants to remain attentive to the trace, the miniscule, the fleeting: "When you speak of a 'wide-eyed presentation of the bare facts,' you are characterizing the genuinely philological stance. This had to be embedded in the construction as such and not only for the sake of results. The nondifferentiation between magic and positivism must in fact be liquidated, as you so aptly formulated it. In other words, the author's philological interpretation must be sublated in Hegelian fashion by dialectical materialists. Philology is the examination of a text, which, proceeding on the basis of details, magically fixates the reader on the text. What Faust took home black on white is closely related to Grimm's reverence for small things. They share the magical element, which is reserved for philosophy to exorcise, reserved here for the concluding part./ As you write in your Kierkegaard book, astonishment indicates 'the most profound insight into the relationship of dialectic, myth and image.' I could be tempted to invoke this passage. Instead I want to propose that it be amended (by the way, just as I plan at another opportunity to amend the subsequent definition of the dialectical image). I believe it should read: astonishment is an excellent *object* of such an insight. The illusion of closed facticity that adheres to any philological examination and that casts its spell on the investigator fades to the degree that the object is construed within a historical perspective. The baselines of this construction converge in our own historical experience. The object thus constitutes itself as a monad. In the monad, everything that was mythically paralyzed as textual evidence comes alive" (Walter Benjamin, *Briefe*, edited by Gershom Scholem and

Theodor W. Adorno, Suhrkamp 1978, vol. 2, pp. 793–794, and cf. Walter Benjamin, *Charles Baudelaire: Ein Lyriker im Zeitalter des Hochkapitalismus*, 1938/1939; in English, *The Correspondence of Walter Benjamin*, translated by Manfred R. Jacobson and Evelyn M. Jacobson, University of Chicago Press, 1994, pp. 587–588).

Notes to Chapter 3

1 In a letter to Kitty Marx-Steinschneider signed in Paris and dated April 15, 1936, Benjamin refers to his work on "the Russian poet Leskov ... a little known but very important contemporary of Dostoyevsky" (*Briefe*, edited by Gershom Scholem and Theodor W. Adorno, Suhrkamp 1978, vol. 2, p. 711; *The Correspondence of Walter Benjamin*, translated by Manfred R. Jacobson and Evelyn M. Jacobson, University of Chicago Press, 1994, p. 525). See the report by the editors of Benjamin's complete works (GS II.3 1277).
2 Toward the end I will return to this concept, which is of primary importance in the thought of Benjamin.
3 The truth content, I mean, and perhaps I should give this idea greater emphasis: it is not only a matter of determinate content that common experience puts at the disposal of participants, as a basis of communication between them. It is a matter of experience as a condition for the appropriation of contents, whatever they may be, provided that one way or another they are effectively communicable. It is in this sense that Benjamin links the loss of the faculty of exchanging experiences—a faculty that the art of storytelling cultivates and develops—with the crisis of experience itself.
4 Georg Wilhelm Friedrich Hegel, *Vorlesungen über die Ästhetik* I, in idem, *Werke* vol. 13, edited by Eva Modenhauer and Karl Markus Michel, Suhrkamp, 1970, pp. 24–25; in English, *Hegel's Aesthetics*, translated by T. M. Knox, Clarendon, 1975, pp. 10–11.
5 See Karl Marx, "Introduction," in idem, *Grundrisse: Foundations of the Critique of Political Economy (Rough Draft)*, translated by Martin Nicolaus, Penguin, 1993, pp. 110–111; also published as an appendix in Karl Marx, *A*

Contribution to the Critique of Political Economy, edited
by Maurice Dobb, translated by S. W. Ryanzanskaya,
International Publishers, 1970, pp. 215–217.

6 See the section "Death as Sanction" in this chapter.

7 I will return to this concept later on, alluding to the formula
that Benjamin uses to define it. See the section "Repetition"
in this chapter.

8 Benjamin himself formulates the exact relationship between
his study on storytelling and the phenomenon of the "fall of
the aura" in a letter written to Adorno on June 4, 1936: "I
recently wrote a piece on Nikolai Leskov, which, without
laying claim to an art-theoretical relevance [he means that
of his essay on the 'Work of Art in the Age of Technological
Reproducibility'], demonstrates some parallels to the 'fall
of the aura' in the fact that the art of storytelling is ending"
(quoted in the editor's comments to "The Storyteller" in GS
II.3 1277; see also Benjamin, *Gesammelte Briefe*, Suhrkamp,
1999, vol. 5, p. 307).

9 Of course, there is a profound and very explicit point of
contact between the two texts. In the Epilogue to "The Work
of Art," which passes judgment on fascism as a general
mobilization of the masses in order to preserve capitalist
property relations, and whose conclusion I have just recalled,
Benjamin speaks of war as the culminating point of "all
efforts to aestheticize politics" and as the essential means
for this mobilization and for the total activation of technical
capacities; and he appeals to Marinetti's *Futurist Manifesto*
as a euphoric and categorical expression of this process
(see GS I.2 506–607, SW IV 269–270). The assessment of
war contained in this Epilogue, apart from the variety of
goals and emphases, is clearly in tune with what he says at
the beginning of "The Storyteller." What is more, after the
emphatic welcome expressed toward technical modernity in
"The Work of Art," no reader will be able to avoid hearing
a bass note that betrays melancholy at the destruction of the
aura and at the loss of the context of tradition into which
that destruction extends its subtle effects.

10 This understanding suggests the possibility of considering
another literary practice, one that certainly does not belong
to the matrix of the epic but is not far removed from it either:

perplexity, lack of counsel, disorientation as a fundamental
mode of existence. These effects can all also be attributed to
another form of writing, which preceded even the appearance
of the novel and has probably been—if we accept Benjamin's
description—the first attempt of the individual to take charge
in this way. I mean the essay. In it—and I think of the first
characteristic form given it by Montaigne, which is no
stranger to storytelling—perplexity is practiced as a tactic
of self-experience and of experience of the world, precisely
on the basis of a crisis of experience, which is not processed
in a skeptical sense and receives its essential definition from
the notion of *essai*. *Experimentum sui* as the core idea of
experimentum mundi, and vice versa, is the character of
an experience that no longer rests on the universality of
knowledge inherited and consolidated in its transmission but
is encountered in an uneasy formative process.

11 If I do not overestimate this point, its importance lies in
showing that, if on the one hand the novel presupposes the
industrial mechanism of print and the mass production that
it allows as its condition of possibility, on the other hand
it continues being defined by the individualized aesthetical
relationship, which technological reproducibility excites
down to the most delicate fiber. In accordance with the
analytic framework of "The Work of Art," the novel acts
as a kind of transition phenomenon between storytelling
and those entirely new forms of narrative that appear in the
second version of the essay on the novel and storytelling and
that Tiedemann and Schweppenhäuser consign to the critical
apparatus of the second volume of *Gesammelte Schriften*
(see GS II.3 1282). Concerning the relationship of the
individual reader with the novel, see "Reading Novels" (in
the last section of "Thought Figures (*Denkbilder*)," entitled
"Little Tricks of the Trade (*Kleine Kunststücke*)" (GS IV.1
436, SW II 728–729). This section develops the analogy
between reading novels and devouring them and proposes
conceiving of the novel as a processing of food, like a kind
of means of cooking a range of experiences that would be
intolerable in a raw state.

12 What I have said about the essay points in this direction, but
it would also be necessary to think about the modifications

that owe as much to the aesthetic reconversion of experiences as they do to the cognitive configuration of the same experiences.

13 See GS II.3 1284–1287, an extensive note (contained in Gershom Scholem's archive) that begins with the sentence "Storytelling is a moral purgative" and its previous stages in the two preceding notes (GS II.3 1282–1284).

14 On this, see Martin McQuillan, "Aporias of Writing: Narrative and Subjectivity," in *The Narrative Reader*, edited by Martin McQuillan, Routledge, 2000, pp. 27–28.

15 Thus Beatrice Hanssen's correct observation that the notion of "origin" that presides over the great work on baroque drama, combined with the discussion of neo-Kantianism and of Nietzsche's eternal return, expresses the aspiration to "nothing less than to think together, and to bring together in one term historical singularity and repetition" (Hanssen, *Walter Benjamin's Other History*, University of California Press, 1998, p. 42).

16 Regarding this, Hanssen quotes the draft of the prologue to *Origin of the German Trauerspiel*, in which Benjamin formulates the idea (see GS I.3 935).

17 With regard to this we might think about the processes of symbolization of death, guided by the desire to remove it from the purely natural dimension of its historical influence. This is also an important theme from the point of view of the theory of sovereignty. Let us recall the affinity between Carl Schmitt's conception in his *Political Theology* (*Politische Theologie*), what Benjamin proposes in the book on baroque drama, and the construction of medieval political theology that Ernst H. Kantorowicz distinguishes as the two bodies of the king, the mortal and the immortal one—which is probably the most complex and carefully articulated way to differentiate between the "historical" and "natural" dimensions of death. See Kantorowicz, *The King's Two Bodies*, Princeton University Press, 1997.

18 See Herodotus, *Histories: Books III and IV*, translated by A. D. Godley, William Heinemann / G.P. Putnam, 1928, p. 13 (= book 3, chapter 10). This story seems to have particularly interested Benjamin. See, besides section 7 of "The Storyteller," the catalogue of various interpretations of the

story (Montaigne, Franz Hessel, Asja Lacis, Dora Benjamin, little Stefan Benjamin, and Benjamin himself) in the last of the "Notes for the Novel and Storytelling Complex" (GS II.3 1288).

19 The difference between the historian and the chronicler reaches its most intense expression in Thesis III of "On the Concept of History": "The chronicler who narrates events without distinguishing between major and minor ones acts in accord with the following truth: nothing that has ever happened should be regarded as lost to history" (GS I.2 694, SW IV 390). Of course, the historian as a figure from whom the chronicler is distinguished is the historian who operates selectively, under the pretense of recounting according to the criteria of historical truth (and of the meaning of history)— criteria that have already been decided upon and firmly grounded. To the extent that chroniclers record in an indifferent manner what the past presents to them, their conduct counts as an expressive example for historical materialists in their debates with historicism and with the ideology of progress.

20 [TN: Indeed, in the *Poetics*, at 1450ᵃ, Aristotle insists that poetic works do not imitate particulars, but "action and life" (*praxeōn kai biou*) and the most important element in what they do is "the arrangement of the incidents" (*tōn pragmatōn sustasis*).]

21 It could be said that this is what allows storytelling in general to survive its death—its end—again and again. While on the one hand the will to end the novel contains in itself the end of storytelling and is perhaps, surreptitiously, a *desire* for this end, on the other hand the paradox inherent in this end contains the constant possibility of resumption, like a more inveterate desire that finds itself in a constitutive discord with the other one.

22 The German term *Märchen* covers a wide range of popular tales, which include the ones we call "fairy tales" [*cuentos de hadas*]. Its etymology is rich but consistent, stretching from news, stories, and rumors to fame, praise, and brilliance.

23 Eric L. Santner, *On Creaturely Life: Rilke, Benjamin, Sebald*, University of Chicago Press, 2006, p. 17.

24 Santner, *On Creaturely Life*, p. 20.

25 On this, see for example the essay "Destiny and Character" (*Schicksal und Charakter*) (GS II.1 171–179, SW I 201–206), to which I also refer in my article "Primeros pasos: *Ethos anthropoi daimon*: Un fragmento de Heráclito y dos lecturas," *Seminarios de Filosofía* 17–18 (2004–2005): 109–131; and the essay "Critique of Violence" (*Zur Kritik der Gewalt*) (GS II.1 179–203, SW I 236–252). See also the notes to my introduction and translation of the latter in *Letal e incruenta: Walter Benjamin y la crítica de la violencia*, edited by Pablo Oyarzun R., Carlos Pérez López, and Federico Rodríguez, Lom, 2017, pp. 17–48.

26 This critique of reason and the demand for an expanded concept of experience emerge explicitly for the first time in the early essay "On the Program of a Coming Philosophy" (GS II.1 157–171, SW I 100–110).

27 Catamnesis would be the inverse of anamnesis or recollection, understood as the return to the beginning. It would be the copy (but nothing more) of the origin.

28 Benjamin formulates his theory of overnaming in the early essay "On Language as Such," which is devoted to his interpretation of Genesis. According to this interpretation, original sin alters the relation of the human being to nature in an essential way. The languages of things, which lack articulate sound, suffer a second muteness, which has a sense of sadness. In this sadness (in all sadness), the creature is at the disposal of the person who names it without being able to communicate its own nature. This is different from what happens with the creative word of God, which calls creatures into existence by their proper name, in the identity of their absolute knowledge. The fallen word can be only a sign that receives its sanction in the bourgeois conception of language. "There is, in the relation of human languages to that of things, something that can be approximately described as 'overnaming (*Überbenennung*)'—the deepest linguistic reason for all melancholy and (from the point of view of the thing) for all deliberate muteness. Overnaming as the linguistic being of melancholy points to another curious relation of language: the overprecision that obtains in the tragic relationship between the languages of human speakers" (GS II.1 155–156, SW I 73). The last indicator

alludes in turn to the signifying that Benjamin bestows on the process of translation (*Übersetzung*), which in "On Language as Such" has the character of a movement or carrying over [*traslación*] from one language to a higher one, through a continuum of transformations (see GS II.1 151, SW I 70; on this idea, see also the first essay in the present volume). This process receives its most rigorous and complex definition in "The Task of the Translator," in terms of an asymptotic relation that has "pure language" simultaneously as its horizon and as its center. Also, on the basis of the "tragic relationship" of human languages (whose meaning is associated with war), the significance that Benjamin gives to storytelling could be understood as a linguistic process that retraces overnaming and its grave consequences.

29 Hanssen, *Benjamin's Other History*, pp. 155–156 astutely notices the reappearance of this theme in Paul Celan's "The Meridian"—the acceptance speech for the Büchner Prize received by the poet in 1960. That piece emphasizes the question of alterity, to which I alluded in passing, and links it to the most original capacity of the poem: "The poem intends another, needs this other, needs an opposite. It goes toward it, bespeaks it./ For the poem, everything and everybody is a figure of this other toward which it is heading./ The attention which the poem pays to all that it encounters, its more acute sense of detail, outline, structure, colour, but also of the 'tremors and hints'—all this is not, I think, achieved by an eye competing (or concurring) with ever more precise instruments, but, rather, by a kind of concentration mindful of all our dates. 'Attention', if you allow me a quote from Malebranche via Walter Benjamin's essay on Kafka, 'attention is the natural prayer of the soul'" (Paul Celan, *Collected Prose*, translated by Rosemarie Waldrop, Routledge, 2003, pp. 49–50).

30 Earlier on I quoted the passage from Thesis II that contains this expression regarding the power of allegory (see n. 15 in Chapter 1 and pp. 61–65 in Chapter 2 of the present volume). Now as well as before, it is worth connecting this power with the *Denkbild* (the thinking image or "image that thinks," as Jorge Navarro Pérez translates it in his Spanish edition of Benjamin's complete works (*Obras completas*,

Abada, 2012). In particular, I evoke "*Florence, Baptistery.*—
On the portal, the *Spes* [Hope] by Andrea di Pisano. Sitting,
she helplessly extends her arms toward a fruit that remains
beyond her reach. And yet she is winged. Nothing is more
true" (GS IV.1 125–126, SW I 471).

Bibliography

Arendt, Hannah. "Walter Benjamin: 1892–1940." In eadem, *Men in Dark Times*. Harcourt, Brace, & World, 1970, pp. 153–206.

Aristotle. *Metaphysics*, translated by W. D. Ross. Clarendon, 1924. Perseus Digital Library.

Aristotle. *Poetics*, translated by R. Kassel. Clarendon, 1966. Perseus Digital Library.

Aristotle. *Rhetoric*, translated by J. H. Freese. Harvard University Press / William Heinemann, 1926. Perseus Digital Library.

Benjamin, Walter. *Arcades Project*, translated by Howard Eiland and Kevin McLaughlin. Belknap Press of Harvard University Press, 1999. [= A]

Benjamin, Walter. *Briefe*, edited by Gershom Scholem and Theodor W. Adorno. Suhrkamp, 1978. 2 vols.

Benjamin, Walter. *La dialéctica en suspenso: Fragmentos sobre la historia*, with introduction, translation, notes, and indexes by Pablo Oyarzun. R. Lom, 1996.

Benjamin, Walter. *Gesammelte Briefe*, edited by Christoph Gödde and Henri Lonitz. Suhrkamp, 1998. 6 vols.

Benjamin, Walter. *Gesammelte Schriften*, edited by Rolf Tiedemann and Hermann Schweppenhäuser. Suhrkamp, 1991. 7 vols. [= GS]

Benjamin, Walter. *Illuminations*, edited by Hannah Arendt, translated by Harry Zohn. Schocken Books, 1968.

Benjamin, Walter. *El narrador*, with introduction, translation, notes, and indexes by Pablo Oyarzun. R. Metales Pesados, 2008.

Benjamin, Walter. *Obras completas*, translated by Jorge Navarro Pérez. Abada, 2012. 11 vols.

Benjamin, Walter. *Origin of the German Trauerspiel*, translated by Howard Eiland. Harvard University Press, 2019. [= O]

Benjamin, Walter. *Selected Writings*, edited by Marcus Bullock and Michael W. Jennings. Belknap Press of Harvard University Press, 1996. 4 vols. [= SW]

Benjamin, Walter. *Werke und Nachlaß: Kritische Gesamtausgabe*, edited by Christoph Gödde and Henri Lonitz. Suhrkamp, 2008. 21 vols. [= WN]

Bloom, Harold. *Kabbalah and Criticism*. Seabury Press, 1975.

Brecht, Bertolt. *Arbeitsjournal*, vol. 1, edited by Werner Hecht. Suhrkamp, 1973.

Brecht, Bertolt. *Bertolt Brecht Journals*, edited by John Willett, translated by Hugh Rorrison. Methuen 1993.

Celan, Paul. *Collected Prose*, translated by Rosemarie Waldrop. Routledge, 2003.

Derrida, Jacques. "Torres de Babel," translated by Carmen Olmedo and Patricio Peñalver. *Er* 5 (1987): 35–68.

Dilthey, Wilhelm. *Introduction to the Human Sciences: Selected Works*, vol. 1, edited by Rudolf A. Makkreel and Frithjof Rodi. Princeton University Press, 1989.

Gadamer, Hans-Georg. *Truth and Method*. Seabury Press, 1975.

Gadamer, Hans-Georg. *Wahrheit und Methode: Grundzüge einer philosophischen Hermeneutik*. Mohr, 1990.

Habermas, Jürgen. "Bewußtmachende oder rettende Kritik: Die Aktualität Walter Benjamins." In idem, *Kultur und Kritik*. Suhrkamp, 1973, pp. 302–344.

Hanssen, Beatrice. *Walter Benjamin's Other History: Of Stones, Animals, Human Beings, and Angels*. University of California Press, 2000.

Hegel, Georg Wilhelm Friedrich. *Enzyklopädie der Philosophischen Wissenschaften im Grundrisse 1830*. *Werke*, vol. 8, edited by Eva Moldenhauer and Karl Markus Michel. Suhrkamp, 1986.

Hegel, Georg Wilhelm Friedrich. *Hegel's Aesthetics*, translated by T. M. Knox. Clarendon / Oxford University Press, 1975.

Hegel, Georg Wilhelm Friedrich. *Hegel's Logic*, translated by William Wallace. Clarendon / Oxford University Press, 1975.

Hegel, Georg Wilhelm Friedrich. *Lectures on the Philosophy of World History: Introduction: Reason in History*, translated by H. B. Nisbet. Cambridge University Press, 1975.

Hegel, Georg Wilhelm Friedrich. *Vorlesungen über die Ästhetik. Werke*, vol. 13, edited by Eva Moldenhauer und Karl Markus Michel. Suhrkamp, 1970.

Hegel, Georg Wilhelm Friedrich. *Vorlesungen über die Philosophie der Geschichte*, vol. 1: *Die Vernunft in der Geschichte*, edited by Johannes Hoffmeister. Meiner, 1955.

Herodotus. *Histories*, translated by A. D. Godley. William Heinemann / G. P. Putnam's Sons, 1928.

Jacobson, Eric. *Metaphysics of the Profane: The Political Theology of Walter Benjamin and Gershom Scholem*. University of Columbia Press, 2003.

Kantorowicz, Ernst H. *The King's Two Bodies*. Princeton University Press, 1997.

Mallarmé, Stéphane. *Selected Poetry and Prose*, edited by Mary Ann Caws. New Directions, 1982.

Marx, Karl. *A Contribution to the Critique of Political Economy*, edited by Maurice Dobb, translated by S. W. Ryanzanskaya. International Publishers, 1970.

Marx, Karl. *Grundrisse: Foundations of the Critique of Political Economy (Rough Draft)*, translated by Martin Nicolaus. Penguin, 1993.

Mate, Reyes. "La historia de los vencidos: Un ensayo de filosofía de la historia contra las ontologías del presente." *Cuestiones epistemológicas: Materiales para una filosofía de la religión*, vol. 1, edited by J. Gómez Caffarena and J. M. Mardones. CSIC / Anthropos, 1992, pp. 183–207.

McQuillan, Martin. "Introduction: Aporias of Writing: Narrative and Subjectivity." In *The Narrative Reader*, edited by Martin McQuillan. Routledge, 2000, pp. 1–33.

Nietzsche, Friedrich. *Die Geburt der Tragödie: Unzeitgemäße Betrachtungen: Kritische Studienausgabe*, vol. 1, edited by Giorgio Colli and Mazzino Montinari. Deutscher Taschenbusch Verlag / de Gruyter, 1999.

Nietzsche, Friedrich. *Untimely Meditations*, translated by R. J. Holling. Cambridge University Press, 1997.

Oyarzun, Pablo. "Un apunte sobre el concepto de experiencia en la *Enciclopedia* de Hegel." *Revista de Humanidades* 8–9 (2004): 139–145.

Oyarzun, Pablo. "Primeros pasos: *Ethos anthropoi daimon*: Un fragmento de Heráclito y dos lecturas." *Seminarios de Filosofía* 17–18 (2004/5): 109–131.

Oyarzun, Pablo. "Sentido, verdad, hermenéutica." In idem, *De lenguaje, historia y poder: Diez ensayos sobre filosofía contemporánea*. Teoría, 2006, pp. 23–76.

Oyarzun, Pablo. "Traición, tu nombre es mujer." In *Ver desde la mujer*, edited by Olga Grau. Ediciones La Morada, Editorial Cuarto Propio, 1992, pp. 143–156.

Oyarzun, Pablo, Carlos Pérez López, and Federico Rodríguez. *Letal e incruenta: Walter Benjamin y la crítica de la violencia*. Lom, 2017.

Plato. *Cratylus*. In vol. 1 of *Platonis Opera*, edited by John Burnet. Oxford University Press, 1903. Perseus Digital Library.

Ranke, Leopold. "On Progress in History." In idem, *Theory and Practice of History*, edited by Konrad von Moltke and Georg G. Iggers, translated by Wilma A. Iggers and Konrad von Moltke. Routledge, 2011, pp. 20–23.

Rosenzweig, Franz. "Scripture and Luther." In Martin Buber and Franz Rosenzweig, *Scripture and Translation*, translated by Lawrence Rosenwald. Indiana University Press, 1994, pp. 47–69.

Santner, Eric L. *On Creaturely Life: Rilke, Benjamin, Sebald*. University of Chicago Press, 2006.

Swift, Jonathan. *Gulliver's Travels*, edited by David Womersley. Cambridge University Press, 2012.

Tiedemann, Rolf. *Studien zur Philosophie Walter Benjamins*. Suhrkamp, 1973.

Index

justice (*cont.*)
 of the journalist xlv–xlvi
 language and xxxiv–xxxv
 meaning of xxxv–xxxvi
 in passive voice xxxiii,
  xxxvi–xxxix, xlv–xlix
 quotation and xliv–xlvi
 split from truth 74
 storytelling 103–7
 storytelling and xx–xxix
 theory/dicaeology 103–4
 truth and 42–3
 "will be done" xl–xli,
  xlvi–xlvii

Kafka, Franz 106
 distortion of existence xli–xlii
 Hebel and xliii
Kant, Immanuel
 concept of history 58
 The Critique of Judgement
  46–7
 experience and 44
knowledge
 becoming of knowing 45–6
 Benjamin's method and 43
 change and 50
 experience and 44
 historical 66–7
 transcendent end 58
Kraus, Karl xliv–xlv, 104

language
 being and 3, 36
 bourgeois conception of 6,
  13, 26, 105
 calling it by its name
  xliv–xlv
 concept of communication
  10–14
 content of 15
 discourse of 38
 growth and 24
 growth of 24

humor and xv, xlii–xliv
justice and xliv, 105
kinship of languages 19,
 26–8
knowledge and 44
law of the essence 14
"of man" xlii
passive voice xxxvi–xxxix, xlii
the passive voice xv–xviii
place of being 26
poetry 18–19
a priori and 32
pure 11, 18–19, 30, 37
quotation xliv–xlvi
radical aspect 2
rhetorical artifices 54–6
specificity 19
speech 30
spiritual being and 4–6, 10,
 11–14
task of theory of 5 *see also*
 communication
 translation
Lask, Emil 48
law
 compared to justice xl–xli
 of the essence 14
Lectures on Aesthetics (Hegel)
 80–1
Leskov, Nikolai xviii, 106
 "The Alexandrite" 99
lexis see discourse/lexis
life
 of artistic works 23, 25
 history and 26
literature *see* novels
 storytelling/narrative
logos
 discourse 38
 mimesis and 7–9
Löwy, Michael
 Benjamin's influence x
Lukács, George
 Theory of the Novel 94